Be a Better Guest

If you're wondering which side of this book is the front, the answer depends on what you want to learn. Open it this way and you're in the guest's seat. Flip it over and you're in the host's chair. Both sides share the same foundations, but your focus shifts with your role.

As a guest, your job is to make your ideas matter; to the host, the audience, and the moment. This book helps you understand how you currently show up as a guest, gives you a simple before-during-after strategy to follow, and offers 30 practical ways to get a little better each time. You'll learn how to prepare in a way that builds confidence and gets your pitch noticed, deliver authentically and with agility in the moment, and make each appearance last well beyond the broadcast, podcast, or panel.

Start here if you have something to share — with your market, your sector, or the world — and you want to share it in a way that feels natural and memorable. This is about positioning yourself without posturing, weaving your expertise into conversations and opportunities, and building a reputation that travels further than the room.

About the Author

Penny Terry has spent more than two decades behind microphones and on stages, shaping, sharing, and shifting conversations that matter. A former ABC Radio presenter, she has interviewed more than 20,000 people, hosted and produced award-winning podcasts, and learned firsthand what makes messages land and what makes them fall flat.

No matter which side of the mic you're on, Penny has lived it in real time. She has experienced what works, studied the evidence, and built clear, practical strategies to help people get better. Today she works with executive leaders, experts, and change makers, helping them share who they are, what they know, and why it matters.

Whether you're asking the questions or answering them, Penny helps you shape the narrative, share it well, and shift what's possible. Because it's not enough to be right, you have to resonate.

Acknowledgement of Country

It would be impossible for me to write a book full of stories without being moved and inspired by the traditions of First Nations cultures.

I acknowledge the palawa/pakana peoples, the Traditional Owners of Lutruwita/Tasmania. I pay my respects to Elders past and present and extend that respect to all First Nations peoples across Australia.

I acknowledge the storytellers and knowledge keepers whose stories are so powerful and so enduring that they have carried vital knowledge of culture, community, and Country through countless generations, sustaining the world's oldest continuous cultures.

I am often reminded of the wisdom in these stories as I walk through the landscapes of Lutruwita/Tasmania. They ground me in the understanding that I live, learn, and work on Country, and they remind me of the responsibility I carry when I share stories of my own.

BE A BETTER GUEST

THE MIC DROP

HOW TO MAKE EVERY APPEARANCE ON PODCASTS, PANELS, AND IN THE MEDIA RESONATE

Penny Terry

Copyright © 2025 Penny Terry

All rights reserved. No part of this publication may be reproduced, distributed, or transmitted in any form or by any means, including photocopying, recording, or other electronic or mechanical methods, without the prior written permission of the publisher, except in the case of brief quotations embodied in critical reviews and certain other noncommercial uses permitted by copyright law.

Every effort has been made to trace and seek permission for the use of the original source material used within this book. Where the attempt has been unsuccessful, the publisher would be pleased to hear from the author/publisher to rectify any omission

First published in 2025 by Hambone Publishing
www.hambonepublishing.com.au

 A catalogue record for this book is available from the National Library of Australia

Editing by Mish Phillips, Lexi Wight and Emily Stephenson
Cover design by I SAW A PLATYPUS
Interior design by David W. Edelstein

For information about this title, contact:
Penny Terry
penny@pennyterry.com

ISBN 978-1-922357-71-7 (paperback)
ISBN 978-1-922357-72-4 (ebook)

Contents

Introduction 1

Going from One in a Million to The Only One 7
    The Ride 7
    The Strategy 13

The Great Toast Theory 19
    The Four Types of Bad Toast 21
    Great Toast: It's Everything You Need and Nothing You Don't 28

Before 29
    The Reccy – Getting the Lay of the Land 32
    The Plan – Create a Map 43
    The Test Run – Practising on Purpose 65
    Set Yourself Up to Shine 73

During 75
    Master Your Mindset – Controlling the Noisiest Guest 78
    In-Of-Body Experience – Staying Present and Engaged 85
    Lift Your Spirit – How to Bring Authenticity to Every Interview 94
    The Art and Science of Showing Up and Being Remembered ... 107

After 109
    The Show Up – How to Keep the Conversation Going After the Mic Turns Off 111
    The Blow Up – How to Make Your Interviews Impossible to Ignore .. 119
    The Glow Up – The Reflection Ritual that Changes Everything 127
    The Conversation That Turns One Moment into Many 134

Conclusion 137
    Then vs. Now 138
    Keep Driving 140

References 143
Acknowledgements 150

Introduction

For years, I sat across from fascinating people — leaders, experts, entrepreneurs — packed with knowledge and experience. They should have lit up the room. Instead, they left us in the dark.

Not because they weren't smart. Not because they didn't have something valuable to say. But because they didn't know how to share it. They were so interesting, yet somehow… so boring.

After interviewing more than 20,000 people, here's what I know for sure: being interesting and being engaging are not the same thing.

I've spoken to experts who could solve global crises, yet their delivery made their insights sound as dull as a telephone book. I've listened to founders with world-changing innovations, yet their explanations made their products instantly forgettable. I've interviewed leaders with visions so bold they could spark a movement, yet their words failed to spark a follow-up question. The problem wasn't their expertise, it was the experience they created.

Not all were like this (and if I've interviewed you, I'm definitely not talking about you, obviously), but more than you'd think.

You might not think being a better guest matters to you right

We live in a world where the loudest voices aren't always the smartest ones.

now, but I'd argue it does. If you know something important, it's more critical than ever to learn how to share that message well. Because it's not enough to be right, we have to resonate.

We live in a world where the loudest voices aren't always the smartest ones. Where influence doesn't always align with expertise. It's not that the best ideas don't exist; it's that they're not being communicated in a way that resonates. You can be right all you want, but if no one hears you, it doesn't matter.

If we want people to listen, engage, and act, we need a strategy. Not a complicated one, a simple one that works. A way to show up, tune in, and make ourselves impossible to ignore.

That's what this book is for.

A while back, I met with a CEO in a café; she was handling multiple media requests each week and she wanted media training. I asked what she was struggling with, and she instantly pulled out her phone to show me the evidence. We then watched a short clip of a recent TV interview she'd done.

Then, the commentary began! She pointed to her own face, saying she looked like she'd been electrocuted. She told me she hated what she was wearing. It was uncomfortable and didn't feel like her. She said she didn't know what to do with her hands, which made her body look awkward. She remembered talking too fast and too much but couldn't remember anything she said. Worst of all, she said she felt silly afterwards.

She told me that experience had made her wary of future media opportunities, concerned about how they might impact her career.

As I listened to her concerns, I looked around the café and thought, *I bet the people at the next table think I'm a dating coach!* Because that's what she was describing – an awkward first date. And therein lies the problem!

Most people treat media appearances, podcast interviews, and panel discussions like a first date. They get all dressed up, often in clothes that don't feel like them. They either overthink every word, risking losing their natural flow, or they spend all their time worrying but never actually prepare. They hope to come across as interesting *and* interested. They try not to look too eager, too arrogant, or too rehearsed. They pretend they know things they don't, and wonder if it is obvious. And then, when it's over, they treat it like a one-night stand – grab their stuff, make a hasty exit, and never follow up!

They *hope* they made a good impression. But *forget* to build a real connection. It's the wrong tactic! To be a great interviewee, you need to treat it less like a date and more like a marriage.

Let me explain.

The Perspective Shift: From First Date to Long-Term Relationship

First dates are about impressions, surface-level charm, carefully chosen words, and planning to avoid risky situations. They're about avoiding awkward silences, trying not to spill your drink, and hoping you don't say something weird that ruins everything.

Long-term relationships are about trust, rapport, ease, a balance of laughs and deep conversations, and knowing how to bring out the best in each other. They're about being comfortable enough to be yourself, showing up consistently, and knowing you'll be invited back because you add something real to the mix.

One-and-done might get you airtime. But resonance? That comes from something more like a relationship. Great guests build relationships with hosts and audiences. They make the conversation feel natural. They leave the host looking good and feeling

It's not enough to be right,
we have to resonate.

great. They get called back, not because they nailed their lines, but because they made the whole experience better.

If you've read books like *Never Eat Alone* (Ferrazzi, 2005) or *Influence* (Cialdini, 1984), you'll recognise that building real relationships, rather than just transactional moments, is a proven path to lasting impact.

The moment you stop treating interviews like one-night stands and start seeing them as the start of something bigger (and better), everything changes.

- You get introduced to their network.
- You get recommended to new hosts.
- You get invited back.
- You become the go-to expert in your industry.

That's how you stop being just another guest and start becoming the guest everyone wants to book. So, which of those two are you now?

Let's find out.

Going from One in a Million to The Only One

How's the chapter title feeling for you? A giant leap? An epic journey? Nah, think of it as a road trip. The best kind of travel, where only adventure-minded people hop in the car.

There'll be pit stops, unexpected detours to places you didn't even know existed, and stop-offs that take longer than you planned; but that's half the fun! You're encouraged to linger at the places that spark your curiosity rather than rushing to the next stop. After all, the best trips aren't about the itinerary; they're about the ride. Strap in.

The Ride

It'd be easy to think that being a good guest is as simple as showing up, answering a few questions, and seeing how it goes. But the ones who get invited back, the ones who get booked on the best podcasts, featured in the media, and sought out for panels and events treat the whole thing differently. They know you only get the full benefit when you stop aiming to be *one of many* and start becoming *the only one worth calling*.

Right now, you might feel invisible, struggling to land interviews, or wondering why the ones you do get don't lead anywhere. Maybe you're getting a few bites, but no follow-ups. Maybe you feel like you're on the edge of being great, but you can't quite figure out what's missing. Maybe you're not interested at all, despite deep down knowing you've got something important to say.

The map below shows the well-beaten path of road trippers who've gone before you. Those who've turned conversations into connections and appearances into opportunities. At each step, you'll see the fuel that's driving you (or stalling you), the weather you're travelling through (a reflection of how things might feel at this stage), and how your message is being received (or not) by others. You'll also see a few signposts to the parts of this book that can help you keep moving forward. Take a look, see where you are on the map, and let's chart your course to where you want to be.

1. You're there out of obligation, you feel invisible, and can sound irrelevant.

Still in the driveway.

You're an expert in something. You've written a book, built a business, launched an idea, gained brilliant expertise, led a great team, or achieved something incredible. But outside your own network, nobody knows who you are.

You're showing up online; posting, sharing, and talking about your work, but it's not gaining traction. Meanwhile, others in your field are being featured, interviewed, and invited onto panels, and you know you could be just as good, if not better.

But you feel invisible, like you're not even in the game and right now, obligation is driving you! Urgh. You're saying what you think you're supposed to say, not what's meaningful or memorable.

You might assume that if you do good work, the invitations will come. But it rarely works that way. Relevance is key.

At this stage, it's not that people are rejecting you. They don't even know you exist.

The Shift to Make: Stop waiting to be discovered. Start positioning yourself to be found.

The Tool to Use: The Reccy. Think of it as your GPS check before you hit the road. It shows you where you are, what sets you apart, and who cares about what you have to say. No more guessing. No more blending in.

2. You're driven by outrage, feel ignored, and it comes across as a rant.

Engine is on, but you're driving solo.

You've started putting yourself out there, because you've decided you've got something to say! You're pitching. You're maybe even landing a few guest spots. But still... nothing sticks. No shares, no referrals, no next-step invites. You're speaking, but the bits you really care about aren't being heard.

Chances are you've stepped up because you've had enough. Outrage is fuelling you, and it shows. You know your stuff. You deserve the mic. But you're coming in hot. The fire's there, but it isn't yet focused. So instead of sparking change, it sounds like you're trying to prove a point. It becomes a rant, not a ripple. The problems are loud, but the solutions don't get heard. You're putting in the work, but you're focusing on the wrong things.

Your pitches are too focused on what you want to talk about instead of what the audience cares about. Your interview answers are good, but they don't spark action. You're answering questions but not shaping conversations. At this stage, you're being ignored and the frustration is real!

The Shift to Make: Stop talking at people and start tuning into people.

The Tool to Use: The Conversation Map. Instead of just answering questions from your soapbox, you'll learn how to shape responses that are clear, compelling, and quotable.

3. You're embracing openness, feeling interesting, and are responsive to the moment.

You're on the map, but not yet bookmarked.

You're starting to get traction. Hosts lean in. Listeners reach out. People start seeing you as *interesting*. Rather than being labelled opinionated, people say, you've got 'an interesting perspective' and that feels like a win. There's a sense of momentum, but it's inconsistent.

One interview feels electric. Another drifts. You walk away from some moments buzzing, and others wondering if anything actually landed. You're present, but still passive.

Now, a sense of openness and adventure is driving you. You're curious, tuned in. You're no longer performing; you're sharing. And when you do? You're shaping the moment, not just surviving it.

The Shift to Make: Stop hoping for a great conversation. Start creating one.

The Tool to Use: The Expert-Ease Factor, so you can stay present, own your voice, and guide the moment without gripping too tight.

4. You see the opportunity, feel in demand and sound refined.

A regular on the road.

You've earned your spot. You're being invited. People know what you bring, and they want more of it. You're not pitching anymore; you're getting pitched to.

But there's a gap. Your interviews are good, but they're not *building*. You're showing up well, but you're not stretching the moment. You're ticking boxes, not turning them into stepping stones.

Now, opportunity is driving you. You see this for what it is: a platform to spring off. You're showing up with a strategy. You're refining your voice, your message, and your delivery.

The Shift to Make: Stop landing moments. Start launching movements.

The Tool to Use: The Show-Up and The Blow-Up. These are strategies for stretching the moment, amplifying your message, repurposing your content, and turning one conversation into ten more.

5. You're taking ownership, feel influential, and are creating resonance.

You're in pole position.

You're not just a guest. You're the go-to voice. You're quoted, reposted, and referred. Hosts shape episodes around you. Your words echo beyond the mic.

At this level, ownership is driving you. You're taking ownership of your voice and your ideas. You know your signal and how to send it out strong. Being a guest isn't a side gig or something you *have* to do. It's your amplifier.

You're not chasing exposure, you're creating resonance. Not just showing up, but shifting how people think, feel, and act.

The Shift to Make: Stop focusing on reach. Ramp up the resonance.

The Tool to Use: The Glow-Up. This is where polish meets presence. It helps you go next-level so your message lingers.

And if you're ready to take the next step? Flip this book. Because the best way to build your platform... is to host one.

Where Are You?

FUEL: What's driving you?	FEELING: How do you feel?	FREQUENCY: How are you received?
OBLIGATION You're speaking up because you feel you should, not because you're ready to shape a message.	INVISIBLE You feel unseen and unsure if anyone's paying attention. What's the point, eh?	IRRELEVANT You're talking, but it's not landing – the message doesn't match the moment.
OUTRAGE You're fired up and ready to be heard.	IGNORED You feel like you're shouting, but no one's listening.	RANTING You've got fire, but no filter.
OPENNESS You're starting to share with curiosity.	INTERESTING You feel noticed. People are leaning in. It's nice.	RESPONSIVE You're tuned in and engaging in real time.
OPPORTUNITY You see this as a chance to grow your reach.	IN DEMAND You feel sought after and busy sharing your voice.	REFINED Your voice is sharp, clear, and meaningful.
OWNERSHIP You know your value and how to deliver it.	INFLUENTIAL You feel powerful, like what you say is shifting thinking.	RESONANT Your words stick and spread.

Where are you on the road trip? Or, better yet, where do you want to be?

You'll notice there are two big lines drawn on this map. The first is the point of no return. Once you get past this, you're off. The second is the go-to line. Cross that and you're officially a go-to voice. This book will help you charge through both.

However, if you're feeling invisible or ignored, you're not alone. Most guests never get past the first few steps because they don't realise there is a system to building this skill. One you can learn. One you can practise. This book will guide you through the strategy that turns one-time guests into go-to voices.

What You'll Get From this Book

Most of these types of books promise to make you effortlessly charismatic, endlessly wise, and bulletproof in interviews. This isn't one of those books. Soz.

Yes, by the time you finish, you'll know how to think on your feet, speak with clarity, and not get cancelled, but that's the outcome, not the focus. The basics of being a great guest are much simpler.

This isn't about learning a whole new skillset; it's about shifting your perspective and applying the skills you already have... in a new setting. Being a better guest isn't about *changing* who we are, it's about *becoming* who we are when the mic, the spotlight, or the moment is ours.

Let's get into it.

Being a great guest doesn't start when the mic goes live, it starts long before we step into the conversation.

The Strategy

The strategy is simple, and once you hear it, it'll feel annoyingly obvious. It has three defined parts. Yet most people only ever focus on one.

- Some over-prepare, rehearsing answers until they sound robotic, but forget to connect in the moment.
- Some rely entirely on being in the moment, then leave with nothing to show for it.
- Almost nobody thinks about what happens after an interview, missing the chance to turn one conversation into many.

To be the guest who gets remembered and rebooked, you need to master all three: before, during, and after.

- Before: know your audience, craft your message, and practise landing your points.
- During: back yourself, stay present, and engage authentically and with confidence.
- After: build relationships, create opportunities, and refine your skills.

Skip any of these? You'll get lost in the crowd. Nail all three? You'll be leading the pack.

Before: Set Yourself Up for Success

Being a great guest doesn't start when the mic goes live, it starts long before we step into the conversation.

Where most guests go wrong:

- They either don't prepare at all, assuming they'll wing it because they 'know their stuff' or have a few talking points (that someone else prepared).
- Or they badly overprepare, cramming their heads with information or scripting answers within an inch of their life.

And even when they do prepare well, most guests still miss the mark because:

- They haven't researched the host or the audience.
- They bring too many points and not enough clarity.
- They don't practise out loud, so their thoughts sound clunky instead of clear.
- They confuse expertise with connection.

The Before section of this book will give you nine tools to help you tune in, prep well, and walk in with clarity, confidence, and control.

During: Own the Moment

Preparation sets us up; however, it's what happens in the room that people remember. Most guests fall apart here because they think their only job is to answer the questions they are asked.

But, as previously discussed (and will be discussed again), being a great guest isn't about delivering words. It's about creating resonance. We do that by speaking *with* an audience, rather than *to* them. Forget about moving information; this is about moving people!

Where it often falls apart:

- Nerves take over: the voice drops, the energy flattens.
- The ramble starts: too many words, no clear landing.
- Hesitation wins: great insights sound like second guesses.
- Overcorrection sets in: it's stiff, formal, and over-rehearsed.
- Connection is lost: it feels like a test, not a conversation.

The wildest part is that most guests don't even know they're doing it, because they never listen back to their own interviews!

The During section of this book walks you through nine ways to hold the (metaphorical) space, stay present, and be the authentic voice people want to listen to.

After: Turning One Conversation into Many

The biggest mistake many guests make is thinking their job is done when the conversation ends. However, finding a way to stick around is what will set you apart.

Where most guests go wrong:

- They vanish: no follow up, no relationship.
- They don't share the episodes: no posts, no tags, no ripple effect.
- They miss the highlights: letting powerful moments get buried inside a 45-minute episode.
- They don't repurpose: leaving insights trapped in a single format or shrivelling on free-to-air broadcasts.
- And they never listen back because, *ugh*, *cringe*, and then nothing improves.

The After section of this book gives you nine ways to turn one conversation into many, build long-term relationships, and turn interviews into long-term assets.

Each of these three sections gives you tools, language, and strategies to help you get to the end of the road trip faster. If you only prepare but don't deliver effectively, you'll be forgettable. If you show up well but don't follow up, you'll lose momentum. If you do all three, you'll be the guest that keeps getting asked back.

So that's the strategy. Sound good? Good. But before we get to that, we need to talk about toast.

The Great Toast Theory

By now, you've probably figured out where you sit on the road trip from One-in-a-Million to The Only One. You've probably started to consider why it's worth your time and effort to make the move over the point of no return and into go-to territory.

You've also started thinking about what needs work, whether it's how you prepare before, how you deliver during, or how you follow up after. You're thinking about the strategy.

But here's what we haven't figured out yet: what actually happens to you when the mic turns on? Because weird things happen when a mic is live. One minute you're an expert, the next you can't remember your name, or suddenly have a corporate accent and use bigger words than you know what to do with. Even the best guests can slip into bad habits without realising it. Chances are, your default settings, the ones you lean on in high pressure situations, are a bit out of whack. The first step is to understand what's going wrong so we know what to tweak. The process isn't too dissimilar to cooking toast.

The Toaster

Years ago, I was standing at a hotel buffet, waiting for my toast to reappear after placing it on the toaster's tiny conveyor belt. While it might look cute, make no mistake, they are rage machines. I'd watched as a guy next to me had already been through the process twice and was growing increasingly frustrated.

First, his toast came out barely warmed. Then, it came out burnt. Then, he then lost his patience entirely. He turned to me and said, "Why can't they build a toaster that gets this right?" And I get it. After interviewing over 20,000 guests, I've realised something: most guests don't come out right either.

Despite their potential, so many of my guests would turn out one of four ways:

- Overdone: stiff, scripted, unnatural.
- Underdone: rambling, hesitant, or hard to follow.
- Slick: they spread it on thick, but it's all style, no substance.
- Dry: technically correct, but with no warmth or spark.

And to mix my metaphors – we've all dated bad toast! We know what bad toast feels, sounds, looks, and tastes like.

As a host, I'm sick of bad toast. As an audience member, so are you. So, I decided to build the toaster.

This book *is* the toaster. It's designed to help you find that perfect balance, where you're prepared but natural, confident but relatable, structured but spontaneous.

Because when you get it right, you become Great Toast. And who doesn't love a great piece of toast?

The Four Types of Bad Toast

You know these people. You've heard these people. You've watched them on TV, heard them on podcasts, and watched them present on panels at a conference. I reckon we've all been each of them at some point, shaped by the moment, the pressure, or the audience in front of us. But which one shows up the most when it's your turn to speak?

The moment you see yourself in one of these, you can tweak your settings and fix it. So, let's break them down, because the difference between forgettable and phenomenal is just a slight turn of the dial.

Burnt Toast: The Overdone Guest

You've heard this one before. It sounds like they're reading straight from a script, or like a grade-six drama student hitting Every. Unnatural. Pause. And totally missing the flow of a real conversation. That's Burnt Toast; over-prepared, over-polished, overdone. Way too stiff. They've rehearsed so hard they can't adjust. If the host takes the conversation in a new direction they can't flex. It's so structured, it's unpalatable (this metaphor is more fun than I imagined)!

Could This Be You?
- You memorise everything and panic if thrown a curveball question.
- You deliver answers like a press release, not a real conversation.
- You sound like you're giving a keynote, rather than having a discussion.

- You're so afraid of getting it wrong that you never actually get it right.

What We Know

Audiences don't connect with perfection — they connect with presence. Who knew? Well, Amy Cuddy did. She says over-preparation pulls us out of the moment. In her book *Presence* (Cuddy, 2015), she explains that when we're overly focused on 'getting it right,' we lose the ability to actually *be there*. It's a bit like when you're trying to remember someone's name and miss the rest of what they're saying.

The Cost

- The host struggles to connect. It's like interviewing a monologue.
- The audience zones out; it's too polished to feel real.
- The guest doesn't get rebooked because they didn't show up, a press release did.

The Fix

- Swap rigidity for flexibility and experiment in low-stakes moments.
- Know your points, not your lines.
- Swap perfectionism for presentism.
- Show up to engage, not to impress.

Raw Toast: The Underdone Waffler

They've got something great to say, they just haven't quite cooked it through. They have the potential to deliver beautiful, authentically (raw) moments, but the lack of preparation means most of these moments get lost in the waffle (a nice breakfast food, but it's not toast). They trail off. They give five half-answers to one question, or jump from thought to thought, leaving the host (and audience) scrambling to make sense of it.

Could This Be You?
- You start with, "Oh, that's a great question..." but never actually answer it.
- You give a mix of half-formed thoughts, hoping one lands.
- You finish a sentence and immediately try to fix it with another one.

What We Know
Structure helps people remember. Concise, clearly structured responses stick far better than rambling ones. Malcolm Gladwell's now-iconic *10,000-hour rule* in *Outliers* (Gladwell, 2008) is often misunderstood, but the core message is clear: deliberate practice matters, and clarity comes from repetition. Which I'm now treating as a disclaimer for anything you feel I'm repeating too often in this book.

The Cost
- The host works overtime trying to extract something valuable.
- The audience gets lost, tunes out and never grasps the point.
- The guest misses the moment – they had the gold, but didn't deliver it.

The Fix
- Pick three key takeaways (only) you want the audience to remember.
- Practise out loud (yes, really).
- Use pause. It shows power, not panic.

Slick Toast: The Guest Who Lays It on Thick

Ever met someone who sounds like they're *always on*? Like they're delivering a TED Talk, a stand-up routine, or a sales pitch, even when they're just answering a simple question? Instead of real conversation, they serve up soundbites, prioritising style over substance. That's Slick Toast. More performer than person, they lean too hard on one-liners, jokes, or forced enthusiasm (insert fake laugh here...).

Could This Be You?
- You laugh at your own jokes but miss the question.
- You drop more names than insights.
- You've got great soundbites but no depth.
- You're on high-energy, but low on authenticity. It feels more like you're playing a character than actually engaging in the conversation.

What We Know

People trust real over rehearsed. When someone's *too* polished, we smell it, and not in a good way. It's like being served a plastic apple: shiny, perfect, and inedible. There are mountains of studies that show that over-rehearsed delivery makes people more sceptical, while genuine moments build trust and credibility. Daniel Pink writes in *To Sell Is Human* (2012) that the best communicators aren't pushing – they're listening, tuning in, and responding to the actual moment.

The Cost
- The audience doesn't trust you. It's all polish, no pulse.
- The host feels like they're interviewing a persona, not a person.
- The guest sounds flashy but is forgettable, as people only remember the performance, not the message.

The Fix
- Dial down the performance, dial up your personality.
- Balance humour with depth; one good insight is better than five average jokes.
- Think resonance, not performance.

Dry Toast: The Guest with All the Facts but No Flavour

Ever listened to someone who's technically fine but completely forgettable? All stats, no spark, just words and numbers strung together. That's Dry Toast.

They get lost in jargon, over-explain, or rattle off facts without thinking about whether the audience actually cares or can even understand them. It's usually not about *what* they're saying, it's *how* they're saying it.

Could This Be You?
- You explain everything perfectly, but no one cares.
- You lose the room halfway through your (very important) data.
- You speak in acronyms and graphs rather than in stories.

You're smart. You're credible. But you're also forgettable, because you don't make people feel anything during interviews.

What We Know

Stories stick. Like glitter. Or gum on your shoe. Depending on who's counting, narrative is anywhere from 13 to 22 times more memorable than facts alone. Carmine Gallo makes the case in *Talk Like TED* (2014) that if you want a complex idea to land, you'd better wrap it in a story.

The Cost

- The audience doesn't feel anything and therefore doesn't remember anything.
- The host struggles to keep the conversation interesting and cuts it short.
- You become forgettable, even when you're right. Grrrrr.

The Fix

- Bring in stories. It's stories that will make your data make sense, and give it meaning.
- Loosen up! Let your personality show, even if it's a serious topic.
- Engage emotionally. If it matters to you, make it matter to them.

A dry, technical delivery might be accurate, but... yeah... I'm bored already.

The best guests find the sweet spot. They're prepared, but not rigid. Confident, but not cocky. Knowledgeable, but still human. Passionate, but not pushy. Informative, but also relatable.

Great Toast: It's Everything You Need and Nothing You Don't

The best guests find the sweet spot. They're prepared, but not rigid. Confident, but not cocky. Knowledgeable, but still human. Passionate, but not pushy. Informative, but also relatable. No pressure... Really, there isn't.

Great toast is about showing up as yourself with what you know. It's the version of you that already knows how to connect, share, and be heard. You do this every day with colleagues, friends, and family without overthinking it.

The key isn't learning something new; it's unlearning what you think is expected. Don't let the toasting process burn away what makes you great. Trust you already have what it takes to be Great Toast; to be someone who can make it matter to *them*, in a way that's unmistakably *you*.

Want to Know Where You Stand?

It's rare that you'll be one type of toast always. Most of us come out differently depending on where we are, who we're with, and what we're talking about. If you'd like to find out where you sit most of the time, scan this QR Code and take my quick quiz. It'll show you what's going well, what's getting in the way, and how to adjust the dial to deliver the gold.

Before

Alright, you've assessed the consistency of your toast, you've mapped the road ahead, and you've wrapped your head around the big picture. Now it's time to shift gears. We're done with theory for a bit. This is where the to-do list begins.

The very first, most important point on that list is this: it's less about what *you* know and more about what *they* know. Your audience.

That's it. If you get that right, you'll be 80% better next time you're interviewed.

Job done. Nearly.

While there are many things you can do before an interview to make you a better guest, writing a media release or memorising some talking points won't cut it (cue the sound of corporate comms teams throwing this book in the bin). I know that's the standard, but it's way out of date. I'm not sure it was ever in date. The conversation *isn't* about your talking points. The conversation *is the point*. Which means there are many more important jobs to do first.

The conversation *isn't* about your talking points.
The conversation *is the point*.

The Eyes Have It

I was working with a client, helping them practise a story for an upcoming interview. As they spoke, I noticed their eyes kept drifting upward, like they were scanning the ceiling for the answers.

Curious, I asked, "What's going on with your eyes?"

They laughed nervously. "I'm trying to read my answers in my head!"

This isn't unusual. When we're nervous or unsure, we often retreat into our heads, trying to recall key lines that we want to say. But when we're focused inwardly and not connecting outwardly, even the right words will sound wrong.

Preparation isn't about memorising words or performing perfectly. It's about feeling confident enough to be present, and we build that kind of confidence by doing the right kind of work before we even step into the room.

"The conversation is not about the thing, it is the thing."

– David Whyte, Life at the Frontier: The Conversational Nature of Reality

The Three Foundations of Preparation

When it comes to being a great guest, preparation boils down to three things:

- Knowing Your Audience: Who are you speaking to? What matters to them? This is about doing your research so you know who you're speaking with.
- Connecting Your Message: It's not just about what you want to say, it's about aligning your expertise with what your

audience cares about. This means you'll be able to share what *you* know, in a way that matters to *them*.
- Practising with Purpose: Saying things out loud, anticipating tricky questions, and visualising success build your confidence and allow you to be present in the moment and deliver your message naturally.

These three steps form the backbone of what we'll explore next. I've given each step a name, because of course I have:

- The Reccy: your go-to for researching like a pro.
- The Plan: the tool to help you shape and land your message, no matter the path.
- The Test Run: how to practise in a way that doesn't suck the life out of your delivery.

When you don't prepare properly, you get lost in the interview – stumbling, second-guessing, trying to find your way. When you *do* prepare well, you lose yourself *in* the interview – fully present, totally clear, completely in it.

Let's get started.

The Reccy – Getting the Lay of the Land

Why The Reccy Matters

On a work trip to Sydney, my sister (and business partner) Lucy and I stepped off the plane, dropped our bags at the hotel, and did what any sensible professionals would do: we ignored our inboxes and calendars.

Instead, we did a Reccy. A reconnaissance.

My gut feeling is that everyone does this when they arrive somewhere new. Am I right, or just me? Basically, we wandered around to get a feel for the place – where to eat, what to do, and how long it would take to get from A to B (though mostly, where to eat).

I reckon every guest needs to do a version of this before an interview. A Reccy helps you get the lay of the land, understand the audience, the host, the topics they care about and decide how best to approach the opportunity. It's not about preparing what you want to say, it's about getting in tune with the host and audience – getting a feel for them.

This kind of preparation is what hosts and audiences notice first – a guest either gets them, or they don't. You want to be the former.

Sounds like common sense, yet I reckon most people skip it. I'd guess fewer than 15% of guests bother with this step.

Let's figure out which percentage you're in.

The Lesson from Rod

Before I explain how to do a Reccy, let's look at what happens when you don't. Not long ago, I received an email from someone pitching to be a guest on my podcast. We'll call him Rod. The subject line read: *Potential Podcast Guest Introduction.*

Now, in my old radio days, I was used to receiving multiple pitches like this daily: press releases, emails, messages, calls from people I didn't know, hoping to get a spot on air. But I don't get as many these days, since I produce niche podcasts with very specific audiences.

Rod's email caught my eye at the time because I was juggling production for three podcasts and needed to fill some interview slots! Here's what he wrote:

Why I would be a good guest for your show:
I believe that discussing the power of handwritten notes would be a fascinating topic for your audience.

Okay, interesting... but there's more.

I can also share my own experiences as a former athlete and sales professional that have shaped my entrepreneurial journey. I believe my background and expertise would provide valuable insights and actionable takeaways for your listeners.

This is a direct excerpt from the email. The problem? The podcast he pitched to is called Rule of Thumb. It's about sexual assault and domestic violence.

Rod hadn't done his Reccy.

Had he done some research, he would have realised that this was not the right show for him. He could have saved his time and mine by pitching to podcasts that were actually relevant to his work. Instead, his scattergun approach damaged his reputation with me (and now you).

Rod's pitch told me three things:

- He didn't care about me or my podcast.
- He didn't care about my audience.
- He only cared about promoting himself.

The result? I didn't just say no to Rod, I mentally blacklisted him. I won't interview him now, nor will I refer him to others.

Why The Reccy Makes a Difference

If Rod had done a Reccy, he would have quickly realised that this show wasn't the right fit for him and saved himself the time and effort of pitching something that was never going to land.

Instead, he could have redirected that energy into researching a program where his expertise made sense. Once he'd found the right show, his pitch wouldn't have been generic, it would have been thoughtful, personalised, and relevant.

Even if Rod wasn't the right fit, a more thoughtful pitch could've landed him a respectful no, or even a referral to someone else. A Reccy would've made that obvious. He would've seen what the podcast was about, who it was for, what tone the host used, and what mattered most to the people listening. That kind of prep changes how your message lands.

Communication researcher Jessica Dziak, who's spent her career dissecting what makes people tune in or tune out, found guests who tailor their message to match the audience's needs don't just sound smarter... they are rated as more likeable, more insightful, and more memorable. Not just by hosts, but by listeners, too. Again, it sounds so very obvious. But believe me, it's not. Common sense is not common, or so the saying goes. Being a better guest is all about relevance. Relevance is what sticks, spreads, and secures your spot as a guest. The people who can do this well can make their topic interesting to anyone.

A Reccy helps you do three critical things:

- Understand the audience, the host, and the platform.
- Tailor your message to connect with them.
- Decide if this opportunity is the right fit.

The Reccy is the first step to being a better guest. So, let's talk about how to do it properly.

Become the Audience

Grab some popcorn — it's time to study the show.

Start by listening to or watching the host's most recent content. What's their rhythm? What kind of guests do they interview? What stories light them up? What's the *tone* of the show? Intimate and slow, or rapid-fire and bold?

I don't expect you to sneak backstage, join the fan page, or get the host's name tattooed on your arm. But you do need to consume at least three of their most recent episodes, shows, or articles – especially any covering your topic.

This will help you understand:

- How the host interacts with guests.
- What kind of stories and angles they respond to.
- The energy, flow, and pace of the conversation.

If I could rename Communication Accommodation Theory by linguist Howard Giles, I'd probably just call it 'Read the Room.' Giles found that when we adjust our tone, pace, and style to match the moment, people often perceive us as more trustworthy, likable, and credible (Giles, 2016). It's not about copying the host, it's about clocking the format, the flow, and the feel, so you can find their frequency, get on their wavelength, and make sure you're on the same page [insert more cliches in here. You don't want to be the guest who's whispering in a nightclub or shouting in a library, so spend some time getting to know their space.

A solid Reccy makes your pitch sharper, your interview stronger, and your message more memorable. It's how you shift from just *appearing* on the show to *belonging* in it.

Try this:

- Consume at least three recent episodes or articles from the show, plus any covering your topic.
- Take note of how the host opens and closes, the types of transitions they use, and what they want from their guests.
- Ask yourself: how did it make me feel as a listener? Was I motivated? Inspired? Entertained? Informed? Did I feel seen?

Make notes on tone and tempo:

- Is it conversational or clinical? Scripted or off-the-cuff?
- Are the interviews tight and host-driven, or open-ended with space to explore?

Track recurring themes:

- What topics come up again and again?
- Where does your expertise intersect or offer a missing piece?
- What angle would feel fresh in this context?

A solid Reccy makes your pitch sharper, your interview stronger, and your message more memorable. It's how you shift from just *appearing* on the show to *belonging* in it.

Know the Front Row

Aussie band The Hilltop Hoods has a song called 'The Nosebleed Section'. The opening lyrics go: *"This is for the heads that's loving the mix, my people in the front all covered in spit..."*

The Hoods know that if you're in the front row at their concert, you're likely to cop a bit of spit. They know what it's like to be their audience.

As a guest, you need to do the same. You need to know:

- Who's listening to this podcast or panel?
- What do they care about?
- What kind of questions are keeping them up at night?

Steven Beebe, one of the world's leading voices in public speaking education, calls this audience-centred communication. He says you can't just build a message and *hope* it lands; you've got to build it *with the listener in mind* (Beebe, 2016). That means understanding their language, their level of knowledge, and the emotional texture of what they're coming for. Otherwise, it's like rocking up to a book club with PowerPoint slides – wrong tone, wrong tools, wrong impact.

Try this:
- Ask: who is this really for? Everyday listeners? Experts? Insiders? What do they already know? What don't they know?
- Create a quick listener avatar: give them a name, a problem, and a goal.
- Scroll through reviews, comments, hashtags — anywhere the audience hangs out.
- Pay attention to how they engage: do they call in, ask questions, shape the conversation?
- Check how the host or event responds to their audience: do they engage, entertain, challenge?

- Spot the patterns: are the audience's concerns practical, emotional, or big-picture?

When you see the audience as more than a mass of ears or eyes, and understand the vibe they've come for, you start to craft something they'll want to hold onto.

Have a Current Affair

If there's one thing I learned from over a decade in the media, it's this: Journalists are having an affair with currency. By currency, I mean your stories don't stand a chance unless they connect to something happening *right now*. Journalists and podcasters aren't just looking for great guests; they're looking for people who can plug into the pulse of what's happening *now*.

Before you get a date on a show, you need to go on a date with the news. Find the threads that link your expertise to what's making headlines, trending, or dominating industry chatter. When you can tie your insights to the conversations people are already having, you're not just more relevant, you're more *bookable*.

This isn't just a media hack, it's a research-backed power move. Back in the '70s, political scientists Maxwell McCombs and Donald Shaw came up with *agenda-setting theory* (*McCombs and Shaw, 1972*). Their big idea? The media doesn't just *mirror* what matters, it *makes* it matter. Like it or not. So, when you link your message to something already in the headlines or floating through the zeitgeist, it's less about adding to the noise, and more about riding the signal. The more timely your take, the more likely it is to land, stick, and get you invited back.

When you can tie your insights to the conversations people are already having, you're not just more relevant, you're more bookable.

Try this:
- Stay in the loop: set up Google Alerts and follow hashtags, blogs, and social threads to keep tabs on what's trending in your space. Although these will probably be out of date by the time this book is published.
- Spot what's unique: notice how others are framing the conversation and find your fresh take, missing piece, or overlooked perspective.
- Make it current: link your insight to a timely news story, industry shift, or hot topic.
- Pitch it well: frame your pitch around relevance. Show how your voice adds something new, needed, and impossible to ignore.

Relevance wins. Always has. Always will. Don't just skim the surface of the show and its audience; dive deep and understand what makes them tick. This level of preparation will make you the go-to in your field much much quicker.

Learning from Legends: Phoebe Waller-Bridge – Matching the Moment

If anyone hacked into my algorithm, it wouldn't take them long to uncover my love affair with the TV series *Fleabag*. As such, the series' writer, actress, and all-round genius Phoebe Waller-Bridge pops up in my feed with suspicious frequency – which, as it turns out, is *very* useful for this bit.

When Waller-Bridge was promoting *Fleabag*, she didn't just roll out the same story everywhere she went. She matched the moment.

On BBC Radio 4's *Woman's Hour*, she slowed right down. The conversation turned reflective and raw, exploring the pressure cooker of societal expectations that birthed her famous character. Waller-Bridge talked about how, back in her twenties, she'd hit a pretty cynical patch, and it felt like, if she looked down into the depths, Fleabag was right there at the bottom, waiting for her. That character, she explained, was born out of all that pressure and self-doubt swirling around at the time (Waller-Bridge, 2019).

But then, turn the dial to *The Tonight Show Starring Jimmy Fallon*, and she's in full mischief mode — leaning into the chaos, cracking jokes, telling hilarious behind-the-scenes stories about filming.

Same show she's promoting. Same core message. Totally different tuning.

That's what the best guests do. They *show up tuned in*.

And yes, I know you know this. Of course you do. It's common sense. But do you do it? Doubt it. I reckon you think you don't have the time. In which case I might ask – if you don't have the time to do this, is it worth your time to do the interview? Just sayin'.

If you do nothing else from this book – do a Reccy.

The Plan – Create a Map

Why Planning Matters

Have you ever been properly lost? I have. Really lost.

Back in 2007, long before Google Maps, my then-boyfriend (now-husband) Barney and I took a trip to California. We were staying near Santa Monica Pier and, being the basic tourists we are, decided we had to see the Hollywood sign. After a few days of wrestling with public transport and taxis, we gave in and rented a car. And not just any car, a black Mustang convertible (because of course we did).

At the car rental place, the attendant asked if we wanted to rent a GPS for $50! It was way too expensive for our backpacker budget, and besides, we had a little map on the back of our hotel brochure, showing the five main arterial roads and a 'You are here' star.

We figured we'd be fine. And things were fine... for about two minutes. Suddenly, there we were, Barney, an Australian, driving on the wrong side of the road, in the wrong side of the car, merging into eight lanes of chaos... and heading straight for Mexico.

I distinctly remember pointing out the back of the Mustang and (very helpfully) saying, *"But we need to go that way!"* It's a wonder we still got married.

I learned very quickly that it's not enough to have a destination; we also need directions to get there.

The same goes for interviews. Having a few talking points is like having a couple of arterial roads and a 'You are here' star. It's not enough. If you want to navigate the twists, turns, and unexpected roadblocks that come your way, you need a proper plan. A proper 'map'.

Planning properly does three critical things:

- Gives you clear directions so you don't end up lost mid-interview.
- Helps you stay flexible so you can handle surprise detours without panicking.
- Makes sure your key points become landmarks instead of getting lost down a tangent.

Let's talk about the three steps that will help you plan your trip properly.

Connect the Dots

When it comes to being a guest, our job is to build a bridge between our expertise and what the audience cares about. If I were Ken Follet, I'd write a whole novel about building that beautiful bridge (if you know, you know).

But let's stick with the road trip metaphor for now. Think of it like packing a bag. If we throw extra things into our suitcase 'just in case', we'll end up with three pairs of swimmers but no toothbrush.

It's the same when we prep for an interview: if we throw everything we know at it, we'll end up cluttered with nothing we need and everything we don't. Your wardrobe (aka: expertise) might be vast, but the audience doesn't need everything, they need the right things. Five show-stopping outfits is all that can fit.

If you want to pack smart, start by connecting the dots.

Try this:
- Write down five topics your audience cares about (based on the work you did in The Reccy).
- For each topic, capture a challenge or problem the audience might say out loud.
- Match each challenge with one of your ideas, key messages, or experiences.

Example:
- **Audience Topic:** Speaking up in meetings, especially when conversations get awkward or tense.
- **Audience Challenge:** *"I feel like I have to talk louder just to be heard, but it never seems to work."*
- **Your Message (or is it mine?):** Rather than turning up your volume, think about how you could turn up your value.

When it comes to being a guest, our job is to build a bridge between our expertise and what the audience cares about.

This exercise ensures you're not just sharing what *you* think is interesting, you're delivering what *they* (the audience) need.

Collect Your Thoughts

Now that you've packed the right things, it's time to plan your route.

When I left radio, I made myself a promise: I'd help guests be better. To sound as good as they are.

I met so many brilliant people with game-changing ideas, but they struggled to deliver them in a way that truly landed. It wasn't a lack of insight; it was a lack of structure. They didn't need to learn more; they needed a way to curate what they already knew so it was ready when they needed it.

That's exactly why I designed the Conversation Map™.

It's like having a map in the glovebox. You might not need to pull it out, but knowing it's there stops you from getting lost.

If you're into classic communication frameworks, you might notice echoes of the *Ladder of Abstraction* (Hayakawa, 1939) or *Transactional Analysis* (Berne, 1964) in here. You'd be right. The Conversation Map is my take on all of that, but built specifically for people who want to share what they know, publicly, in a way that lands. It's grounded in solid science, but made for real conversations, not textbooks.

There are a couple of extra layers I add in other contexts, but for now, this version gives you exactly what you need to be a guest who shares insight *and* creates connection.

It also borrows from some other useful techniques and formats that I love.

Memory champions use a technique called *Memory Palaces* to structure and retrieve information with ease (Yates, 1966). The Conversation Map works on the same principle, organising your thoughts beforehand so they're easier to recall under pressure. And it's not just about memory. Cognitive Load Theory tells us that our working memory can only juggle so much at once (Sweller, 1988). When you have a structured way to store information, your brain isn't wasting energy rummaging around for the right words.

I've also been influenced by Matt Church's structured approach to idea development in *Think* (Church and Cook, 2018) and how he's captured a process on one page in his *Pink Sheet*. It's game-changing.

Importantly, The Conversation Map isn't about scripting. It's about storing your key points in a way that's ready to roll when the moment comes so you'll have the right words, at the right time, for the right audience.

How to Build Your Conversation Map

You can create a Conversation Map for each key message, theme, or the entire interview. It's up to you. The goal is to shape your message so it's *easier to say and harder to forget*.

Here's how it works.

SUGGEST – The Reframe – Start with a big idea.

Think of this as your North Star, the key theme that everything else revolves around, and when done well, flips the focus from the get-go. It should be simple, repeatable, and instantly clear.

For example, if you're talking about workplace communication, your frame might be: *"For me, it's all about connection."* This isn't the quote (yet), it's the idea that anchors the conversation.

Psychologists call this 'framing', how you set the context for what's to come (Fairhurst and Sarr, 1996). It's why two people can talk about the same topic but leave vastly different impressions. The way you frame your idea shapes how others interpret and remember it. The person who wraps their idea up in relevance wins.

In the media, we call this headlining, boiling a complex idea down to something clear, sticky, and worth talking about. If you don't headline yourself, someone else will, and it might not be the story you want told.

REFLECT – Their Belief – Identify a challenge or belief your audience already holds.

The fastest way to get people to listen? Say something they're *already thinking*.

For our workplace communication example, you might say:

"People tell me they feel ignored. Sometimes it's because they don't feel confident enough to speak up. Sometimes it's because they've spoken up before and no one listened. And sometimes, it's because only the loudest voices seem to get airtime where they work."

Suddenly, heads start nodding. Your audience sees themselves in your words, which makes them lean in. People don't lean in because you hit them with the facts; they lean in because you say something they already believe but hadn't quite put into words yet.

Jiyeon So and Hyunjin Song found that when speakers reflect their audience's real frustrations, engagement and comprehension don't just rise, they *take off* (So and Song, 2023). First, we need to show people we're on their wavelength, and then we'll earn the right to take them somewhere new.

It's the difference between forcing an idea onto someone and guiding them toward a realisation they already feel is true. You're tuning into their frequency first, and slowly getting them ready to switch stations with you.

People don't lean in because you hit them with the facts; they lean in because you say something they already believe but hadn't quite put into words yet.

RESPECT – Their Experience – Why this belief exists.

Now that you've connected with your audience's belief, the next step is to show them why they feel that way, and why it makes complete sense.

For our workplace communication example, if the belief is "I feel ignored", the next step is to validate their experience, not shame it:

"And that makes sense, because most workplaces reward the voices that take up space. If you've ever been talked over, dismissed, or had your ideas ignored, of course you'd start believing that speaking up isn't worth it."

It's not about agreeing with their stuckness, it's about showing you understand *how* they got there. That moment of respect and recognition builds trust.

Back in the 1950s, Leon Festinger coined *Cognitive Dissonance Theory*, which basically showed that if you try to change someone's mind before showing you get them, they dig their heels in (*Festinger, 1957*). But when you acknowledge their reality first, things soften. The ground steadies. They don't feel challenged, corrected, or shamed, they feel seen.

CONNECT - Their Currency - What's the thing that drives them?

After you've validated their experience, it's time to connect with that thing that really matters to them - the thing they're investing in. It could be time, energy, recognition, growth, well-being or money.

For our workplace communication example, if the belief is "no one values what I bring," the next step is to show that you get what that's costing them. You might say, "Being recognised for your contribution and knowledge is a huge driver for many people." In leadership research, this kind of exchange is known as Leader–Member

Exchange (Graen & Uhl-Bien, 1995), the idea that relationships thrive when both sides feel the trade is fair. As a guest, it's about acknowledging what people are putting in - their time, energy, or reputation - allowing trust and cooperation to rise. By naming that unspoken trade, you build credibility, connection, and the kind of influence that lasts.

SHIFT - Your Perspective - What's the quotable takeaway?

This is your wisdom bomb, the one-liner that sums up your message in a way people can remember and repeat.

For our workplace communication example, the key message might be: "Yelling only makes you louder, not easier to hear".

Messages like this stick because they're simple and tell a deep truth. They're different to opinions. While opinions reveal something about us, perspectives reveal something about the audience. That's what makes them repeatable. Jonah Berger found that ideas spread when they're memorable, useful, and make people feel good when they pass them on, especially if sharing them makes them look smart, kind, or in-the-know (*Berger, 2013*). Your job is to give people a line they'll want to quote.

If a host or audience member can drop your message into a conversation later, without needing notes, you've nailed it.

SHOW - The Story - The moment that makes it real.

If your quotable message is what grabs attention, your story is where you make it matter. I love stories (and honestly, I can't let myself go all in here, as we'd need a whole other book). But here's the short version: stories aren't about dazzling people; they're about helping them *believe* you. A good story gives your audience something to hold onto. It turns your point into a picture. It transforms an

While opinions reveal something about us, perspectives reveal something about the audience.

idea into something they can see, feel, and remember. Importantly, it rewrites the experience (see above) that informed their unhelpful beliefs.

Uri Hasson and his team found that when we hear a story, our brainwaves sync up with the storyteller's through a seemingly magical process called *neural coupling* (Hasson et al., 2012). Woah. Plus, if you want to be remembered, Chip and Dan Heath found that stories are 22 *times* more memorable than facts alone (*Heath and Heath, 2007*).

While I firmly believe that we are all storytellers, don't let the weight of that word put you off. Swap out story for example. You just need to give your audience a lived moment that helps them make sense of what you mean. That's when a message becomes more than words, it becomes something they can carry.

There are lots of ways to tell a good story. But let's keep it simple, proven, and ready-to-use. Here's the structure I trust most:

- **Beginning** – Set the scene.
- **Middle** – The guts of your story. Use concrete details that illustrate your message. Add in some tension if you can.
- **Bridge** – The link. As the ever-brilliant storytelling guru Gabrielle Dolan explains, this is the part that *connects* your story to your point (Dolan, 2017). A simple half-phrase like, "What I remember thinking in that moment was..." will go a long way.
- **End** – Land your key message. This is the same message you shared above, phrased differently.

The best stories are short, sharp, and structured. If you ramble, your audience tunes out. And while not every opportunity allows time for a full story, most do, if you know how to keep it tight. That's why you need to practise telling your stories at different lengths: 15 seconds, 30 seconds, 60 seconds, and 90 seconds. The better you get at shaping them to fit the moment, the easier they'll come when you need them.

CITE – The Evidence – Back it up.

While I love stories, I love evidence equally. If stories captivate, data validates. That is, stories hook people emotionally, and evidence convinces them logically. A great message balances both.

For our workplace example:

"The research tells us that repeating the same message over and over can actually make people tune out. But when you adjust how you say it based on who's listening, they're far more likely to engage and remember it." Better still, reference the study or researchers (in this case Jiyeon So and Hyunjin Song), share a powerful stat, or quote an influential voice in the field.

It's less about being smart, and more about being strategic. According to persuasion researchers Richard Petty and John Cacioppo, we take in messages two ways: through our hearts and through our heads (Petty and Cacioppo, 1986). The best guests can spark a feeling *and* satisfy the logic check in each answer.

LIFT – Their Dream – What's the goal they're aiming for?

It's time now to bring it back to what this is all about - the outcome you're helping them move toward.

In our communication example, you might say: "Because when people they're being heard, that's when high-impact work happens." Edwin Locke and Gary Latham, the godfathers of goal-setting theory, spent decades studying how goals drive performance.

They found that when people have a clear sense of what they're working toward, focus sharpens, motivation lifts, and the work suddenly means more (Locke & Latham, 2002). The clearer and more meaningful the goal, the greater the commitment to reach it. So when you connect your idea to the outcome your audience already cares about, you're showing them that your idea takes them where they want to go.

DIRECT – The Action – What's the next step?

This is your baton pass, what you want your audience to do next. Don't forget this step, please. It could be:

- A simple tip they can use immediately.
- A challenge to test in real life.
- A resource, tool, guide, or website to explore.

For example:

"Next time you're in a meeting and feel like you're not being heard, rather than repeating your point, try reframing it. "What if it's not about x and it's actually about y?" and then watch what happens.

Behavioural scientist Susan Michie found that inspiration is great, but without one clear, simple action step, most people will do absolutely nothing (Michie, van Stralen, and West, 2011). Turns out 'seize the day' needs a calendar invite.

Your Ultimate Collection

A completed stack of Conversation Maps is like your 'Best Of' album. You know all the lyrics words. You hit every note. And when you share them well, everyone else starts singing along. The tunes are clear, catchy, and impossible to ignore.

Try this:

Normally, this part comes with flip charts, butcher's paper, and me asking you to sit next to someone you haven't met yet (kidding, I'd never do that), but you don't need a workshop to get started. Here's a simple exercise to kick your Conversation Map off.

Set up a simple grid like the example on the following page, with the headings down the left-hand side, anc put your words down the right-hand side:

The Step	Your Words
SUGGEST The Reframe: Provide a new way of thinking about the topic. This is your big idea or North Star.	
REFLECT Their Belief: What does the audience already feel, experience, or believe?	
RESPECT Their Experience: Explain why the belief exists. Respect it. Validate it.	
CONNECT Their Currency: Connect into that thing that drives them. The thing they're investing.	
SHIFT Your Perspective: What is the quotable takeaway? One line to rule them all.	
SHOW The Story: Share a moment that makes your message meaningful, rewriting their existing narrative.	
CITE The Evidence: Provide a stat, fact, or quote to back up your story.	
LIFT Their Dream: Remind them of the goal they're aiming for.	
DIRECT The Action: Share one simple thing your audience can do next.	

While this table makes it look linear, it's not. These are key points on a map that you can visit in any order you like. There is no 'right' way or route you should take. This is a road trip, not a guided tour, and this map gives you the confidence you need to go with the flow.

Tick the Boxes

In the novel *The Rosie Project,* Australian author Graeme Simsion tells a beautiful story of a professor who creates a questionnaire to find the perfect girlfriend – a logical, methodical way to assess compatibility. If hosts did the same thing, which officially we don't (but unofficially, maybe, we do), we're also assessing compatibility.

The novel explores the idea that the best connections rarely come down to what's on paper, but let's be honest: it's still where a lot of people start, whether they mean to or not.

From the get go hosts, editors and organisers are assessing if you're a risk or an asset to their show, publication, or event. You're aiming for the latter. And if you don't tick their boxes? You probably won't get booked.

Let's go through the boxes that you need to tick.

Content – Is Your Message Relevant, Current, and Personal (or Exclusive)?

Hosts don't want generic guests. They want people who have something fresh to say. If your topic isn't timely, relevant, or unique, it won't stand out – no matter how important it feels to you.

Podcast strategist Alex Sanfilippo has seen it over and over again: the guests who get booked (and rebooked) are the ones who bring something timely, tailored, and a little bit extra. Not just 'Here's what I want to talk about', but 'Here's why your audience needs this *right now*, and why *your* show is the place to do it.'

He calls this the key to being a *high-value guest*, and frankly, it's how you go from inbox pitch to podcast (*Sanfilippo, 2023*). This where you put all those work you did in The Reccy to work.

Try this:
- Make it timely: get clear on how your message aligns with what this audience cares about *right now*.
- Make it fit: it should make a host immediately see why *you* make sense for *them, and their show, right now*.
- Make it exclusive: offer a bonus – an insight, a story, a download, a giveaway – something the host (and their audience) can't get anywhere else.

Now, pull those three things into one clear sentence you can say out loud. You'll use it in pitches, bios, intros, even over coffee.

Character – Are You Informed, In Tune, and Interesting?

Being a great guest isn't just about *what* you say, it's about *how* you say it. You could have the best insights in the world, but if you sound flat, hesitant, or disconnected, the audience won't care. This is about ticking the *Golden Toast* box.

Let's defer to the big guns for a moment. Terry Gross, host of *Fresh Air*, is famous for coaxing out the real person behind the persona. She doesn't want guests to perform; she wants them to show up as themselves (Gross, 2018). And Ira Glass, host of *This American Life*, says the best guests are those who talk like themselves, quirks and all, and in a voice that's unmistakably theirs, not like a press release on legs (Glass, 2007).

Make this obvious from the get-go. Pitching isn't about rattling off your résumé; it's about letting your real self shine through. The host wants to meet you in the pitching process, not just your talking points.

Try this:

- Show what you know: drop in a sharp detail that proves your experience or perspective without needing to say, 'I'm an expert.'
- Show you get them: reflect the vibe, tone, or values of the audience you're speaking to. It should feel like you belong in the room.
- Show you're real: share a quick moment, story, or lived example that brings your message to life. If you say you're 'passionate' and leave it at that, you've already lost.

Now, write one sentence that shows who you are — not with labels, but with proof. Use it in your intro, your bio, or your pitch. Let them hear you *before* you speak.

Capacity – Are You Findable, Flexible, and Comfortable Behind the Mic?

You'd be surprised by how many people put out media releases, then disappear or aren't available for interviews. Or agree to interviews they're not ready for. Don't be that person. Production and editing teams are racing tight timelines, rolling news cycles, and last-minute changes. They want guests who are easy to book and easy to work with.

Producer and podcast host Jay Acunzo says his favourite guests are the ones who are *a breeze to work with*. They show up on time, with something good to say, and make post-production easier, not harder. Being brilliant is great, being reliable *and* brilliant? That's what gets you rebooked (*Acunzo, 2021*).

Try this:
- Be findable: make sure your online presence is up to date, so when someone Googles you, they find the right you and know how to contact you easily. A 'contact us' form won't cut it.
- Be flexible: if you can offer scheduling options, quick turnarounds, or tech setups that work, say so.
- Be ready: prove you're comfortable on mic. Mention past interviews, panels, podcasts, anything that shows you're not afraid of a blinking 'record' light.

Now, write one sentence that shows you're low-maintenance and mic-ready. Hosts remember the guests who make their lives easier.

Getting the Plan Done

So that's how you plan.

- Connect the Dots: make sure your message aligns with what the audience cares about.
- Collect Your Thoughts: outline your key message, story, and call to action.
- Tick the Boxes: show that your content is valuable, you're engaging, and you're easy to work with.

When you plan your trip properly, you're ready for any detour, and your audience will want to come along for the ride.

Learning from Legends: Michelle Obama – Map It, Don't Script It

Yep, we're going there. When you think about it, Michelle Obama spent the better part of a decade being a professional guest. Interviews. Panels. Community events. Town halls. Every week, sometimes every *day*, often multiple times a day, stepping into other people's spaces, answering other people's questions.

You might think she had a script tucked up her sleeve. And for the big speeches, she did. In her book *Becoming*, she explains how her team would spend weeks shaping those moments to reflect her values and meet the moment. That's big-stage stuff.

But when it came to being ready for real conversations, she had a different strategy. She explains that when she's asked to speak off the cuff, she often draws on real stories from her own life-moments she's lived, rather than scripted lines (Obama, 2018). That's a sign of a clear internal map.

She knew her frames, her messages, her stories. She didn't rehearse them word-for-word, she just *organised* them. So, when the moment came, she could reach for connection instead of scrambling for the right words.

And Michelle Obama followed every part of The Plan:

- She **Connected the Dots** by making her messages personal and relevant, always tailored to the audience in front of her.
- She **Collected Her Thoughts** by building a mental library of real moments she could pull out as needed, ready, but never robotic.
- And, whether she meant to or not, she **Ticked Every Box**. Her content was powerful and current. Her character

The only way to know if your words work is to say them aloud. Not in your head. Not in bullet points. Full sentences, out loud. You've got to feel them in your mouth.

was grounded and human. And her capacity? Next-level. She showed up prepared, poised, and present every single time.

Let me be clear — you don't have to be Michelle Obama to get this right. You just need to plan like someone who cares about the conversation, not only the mic.

The Test Run – Practising on Purpose

I know you were wondering. The answer is, *Yes, you need to practise*. But practising is very different from memorising. Let's work through it.

Why Practising Matters

Whenever I go to a wedding, there's one part of the ceremony that always makes me nervous. It's the moment someone starts walking down the aisle. I hold my breath, hoping they'll reach the front right as the song finishes, not before, with a weird fade-out, and not after, with awkward silence. Just perfectly, seemingly magically, timed. And it's not just weddings, I do this everywhere.

If you've ever listened to my podcasts, you'll hear the music wind up exactly as I stop talking. That's years of radio training. I reckon it feels like magic when the timing's right. Did I nail it at *my* wedding? You bet I did. But it wasn't magic. It never is. It was rehearsal. We did a test run.

The same applies to being a great guest. If you want to nail your interview, land your ideas cleanly, and leave your audience with that same satisfying, magical feeling, you need to do a test run too.

It's this step that builds confidence and familiarity, the antidote to going blank.

> *"The fight is won or lost far away from witnesses, behind the lines, in the gym, and out there on the road, long before I dance under those lights."*
>
> - Muhammad Ali

A little preparation goes a long way. Once the mic is on, you don't want to be figuring it out on the spot, you want to make like Muhammad Ali and land the punch or, in our case, land the point.

To get it right, there are three things to focus on:

- **Say It Out Loud**: find out how the words feel coming out of your mouth.
- **Build a Safety Net**: have a plan in place for anything you're worried about.
- **Visualise Success**: do a mental rehearsal of the whole thing.

You don't need to show up perfect, you need to show up practised.

Say It Out Loud

The only way to know if your words work is to say them aloud. Not in your head. Not in bullet points. Full sentences, out loud. You've got to feel them in your mouth.

There's a massive gap between how something sounds in your head and how it lands when you speak it. Ever written an email that made perfect sense, until you read it out in a meeting? Exactly. Same thing happens in interviews.

What looks sharp on paper can sound clunky when spoken. Rhythm changes. Emphasis shifts. Suddenly, a smooth sentence that felt effortless when written feels awkward when spoken.

David Goldinger, who studied speech recall and fluency, found that saying things out loud, even once, makes it easier to retrieve ideas under pressure (Goldinger, 1996). The more you externalise your ideas, the easier they are to shape naturally in conversation.

Try this:

Find simple, everyday ways to practise speaking your key points out loud:

- Practise while driving: talk through your key points in the car. No one's listening, so just let it flow. It's the easiest way to get comfortable speaking out loud without overthinking it.
- Chat with AI: use the voice function on your favourite AI assistant and prompt it to ask you questions in the style of your interviewer. Instant practice, zero judgment.
- Answer your own questions in voice notes: use your phone's voice memo app to record yourself answering key questions. Play it back and notice what works and what doesn't.

Even if you prefer to speak off the cuff, saying things out loud, just once, makes a huge difference in how confident you'll sound when the mic goes live.

Build a Safety Net

One of the biggest fears I hear from clients is, "What if I don't know what to say?" In my experience the fear has little to do with not having the answer and more to do with the panic of their mind going blank.

Enter: planned spontaneity. Robin Rickards, Canadian community advocate and author coined the term in the early 2000s (Rickards, 2000), and it's perfect. It means preparing a few tools ahead of time that help you *feel* spontaneous even when you're not. Think of it like carrying an umbrella: you might not need it, but knowing it's there stops you from worrying about the rain.

By preparing just a few simple phrases, you give yourself a safety net, a way to pause, reset, or redirect the conversation without fumbling. Most of the time, just knowing you have these tricks up your sleeve is enough to quell the anxiety, whether you ever need to use them or not.

Sentence Starters

Silence in an interview can feel louder than it is. In that panic, people often say things they wish they hadn't. Instead of scrambling, have some sentence starters ready to go. You could try:

- "That's an interesting question. What's coming to mind is..."
- "I can see why you'd ask that. The way I look at it is..."

These give you a second to breathe while keeping the energy moving. And if you don't know the answer? Say so. I hereby give you permission!

- "I don't think I've got a great answer for that — but now I'm curious, so I'm going to find out."

Clarifying Questions

More often than not, when I'm listening back to an interview with a client, there's a moment where they say, *"I wasn't sure what they meant by that question, so I just guessed..."*

Don't guess. Ask. Interviewers are human. They sometimes ask vague or broad questions. Instead of guessing and hoping for the best, ask for clarification. Please. You're allowed. You could try:

- "What specifically are you interested in?"
- "I'm not sure I understand. Could you rephrase that?"

Contrary to what you might be thinking, this doesn't suggest you're not listening, it doesn't suggest you don't know your stuff, but rather, it shows you're engaged and want to give a relevant answer.

Bridging Statements

Sometimes an interviewer heads somewhere unhelpful. Wrong angle. Wrong assumption. Off-topic, for you. Rather than shutting it down or fumbling, have a bridging phrase ready to gently steer things back on track.

They are short statements that help you guide the conversation back to your key messages without ignoring the question. But, use them sparingly. If you overdo it, you'll sound like a politician trying to dodge a question. You could try:

- "While people often ask about that, I've found what they really want to know about is..."

- "What I'm really keen for people to understand is..."
- "That's not something I'm able to talk about, but what I can say is..."

Bridging keeps the conversation on track without sounding forced.

Try this:
- Write out three sentence starters, three clarifying questions, and three bridging statements that sound like something you would say. Use your language (not mine).
- Practise saying them out loud so they feel natural, find their spot in your brain, and are ready to go!
- Print them out and take them with you, or stick them up on the wall behind your computer.

Even if you never use them, knowing they're there if you need them will make you feel more confident and prepared for any detour.

Visualise Success

I love science. Apparently, picturing yourself doing a thing can actually make you better at doing the thing. Mind blown.

Performance psychologist Thomas Driskell and his team found that *mental rehearsal* can lead to big improvements, sometimes just as powerful as physical practice (*Driskell et al., 1994*). Golfers who visualised their shots before swinging improved by 30%. The same effect's been seen in surgeons (thankfully), musicians, and elite athletes. I haven't (yet) run the experiments on podcast guests... but I'm pretty confident the same brain magic applies.

Why it works:
- Visualisation activates neural pathways linked to the skill, so your brain gets practice before you actually do it.
- It reduces anxiety because mentally rehearsing makes the experience feel familiar.
- It sharpens performance, your brain starts recognising what 'nailing it' looks and feels like.

Try this:

Take five minutes and imagine yourself in the moment, from start to finish:
- Arriving at the studio, on stage, or logging into the interview.
- Getting in sync with the interviewer with some friendly banter.
- Hearing the first question and answering confidently.
- Smiling as you finish, knowing you nailed it.

It might feel weird at first, but that's just your unfamiliarity speaking. The more you tune in to that picture of success, the more your brain believes you're already there.

Wrapping Up the Test Run

Before your next interview, take the time to run a test. It's about feeling ready. When you do a test run, you don't just prepare your words, you prepare yourself. And that's what allows you to show up present, engaged, and natural when the mic goes live. This is how it works:
- Say it out loud: get to know what the words feel like to be said rather than written, or record yourself speaking, then review.

- Build a safety net: prepare sentence starters, clarifying questions, and bridging statements.
- Visualise success: picture yourself walking in, speaking confidently, and finishing strong.

A little preparation goes a long way.

Learning from Legends: Brené Brown – Practised, but Present

Brené Brown didn't just magically know how to do interviews when she got famous. When her TED Talk exploded and *Daring Greatly* hit the shelves, she found herself catapulted into the world of live TV, panels, and media spots and it wasn't smooth sailing. She's talked about how she had to learn to stay true to herself once the cameras were on, because it's surprisingly easy to lose your sense of authenticity when you're focused on getting everything 'right' (Brown, 2020).

That's what makes Brené the ultimate test run role model. She didn't practise to be perfect. She practised to stay present, even when the lights were blinding and the stakes felt sky-high. In *Daring Greatly*, she backs this up, writing: "We have to practise showing up even when we can't control the outcome" (Brown, 2012). And honestly, is there a better description of being a guest?

Brené's interviews aren't polished to the point of perfection. They're thoughtful. Sometimes a little messy. Always real. Because she's done the prep work behind the scenes, she can tune into the moment and not panic when things get vulnerable, weird, or off-script.

And that's the real point of a test run. Not to get every word perfect. But to build the reflex to show up as you, even when it would be easier to duck and run.

If even Brené Brown had to practise showing up without losing herself, I reckon we're all allowed a few test runs before we find our real signal, too.

Set Yourself Up to Shine

So, you've now done the groundwork to move from being one in a million to the only one, from invisible to influential, from just another expert to the go-to voice in your field. You've learned that being a great guest starts long before the mic is on. It's not just about showing up, it's about showing up ready.

Here's what you've locked in:

- The Reccy: you now know how to research like a pro, so you're never out of place, off-topic, or pitching to the wrong audience.
- Plan the Trip: you've mapped your expertise to what the audience actually cares about, so you can group your key points and make your message land every time.
- The Test Run: you've built a safety net and a practice process so when the moment comes, you're ready for anything.

This work stops you from being underdone or overdone. No more raw toast that waffles without direction, and no more burnt toast that sounds too scripted and stiff. Instead, you're on your way to being Great Toast; engaging, natural, and impossible to ignore.

The Moment You've Prepared For

And now, it's time for the real test: what happens when the mic is live?

This next section is about what to do *while you're speaking*: how to keep the conversation flowing, land your key points in real time, and make the kind of impression that sticks.

Because being prepared is one thing, but delivering in the moment is what makes you stand out proper.

During

You've done the prep, you've made the plan, you've run the test. Now comes the part that separates forgettable guests from great ones.

This is where most people stumble. Then the mic goes on, and your mind goes blank. You freeze. You forget your key points. Your face looks terrified. You awkwardly share details that aren't important, or are barely appropriate. You catch yourself thinking about the last answer while you're answering the next one. Plus, you're talking with a weird corporate accent.

I see this happen all the time. While good preparation gets you to the starting line, it's a different set of skills that are needed once the mic goes live. The good news is, you already have these skills; we just need to unlock them. Luckily, I've got the key!

The Key:

So many people ask me about confidence. They want to know how they get it, as if they might pop down to the shops and buy a packet of confidence. Confidence isn't something you're born or blessed with, nor can it be bought. Which, I know, is terribly disappointing. It certainly doesn't come from perfection, how could it? It comes from repetition.

My mash-up of multiple quotes on confidence is: confidence isn't the absence of nerves, it's the presence of trust.

To build that trust, you need to do some strength and conditioning training. You don't wait to feel strong to lift the weights, you lift the weights to feel strong. Confidence works the same way. You build it through reps, not reassurance.

That means working three key muscles: your mind, your body, and your spirit. Each one plays a different role in helping you stay grounded, connected, and unmistakably you when the pressure hits.

Here's how you do it:

- Master your mindset: the conversation in your head shapes the one outside of it. Take care of the former and the latter will take care of itself.
- In-of-body experience: yep, we need to practise staying *in* our bodies when the mic is on. It's about how we sit, breathe, and move.
- Lift your spirit: pressure can make even the most authentic people feel stiff, scripted, or disconnected. This is about knowing how to lift up your authentic self into high-pressure situations.

Each of these shifts will help you stop performing and start connecting. So, you'd better come into the studio.

Confidence isn't the absence of nerves, it's the presence of trust.

Master Your Mindset – Controlling the Noisiest Guest

You'd think that after ten years behind a mic, I'd make a pretty good guest. You'd be wrong. Spectacularly wrong.

I remember walking into my old studio for my first interview as a guest, rather than as the host. My good friend and former colleague was sitting opposite me. I had everything going for me. I'd done all the prep. I knew how to map my message, and I had. I knew how to speak clearly, with years of practice. I was as comfortable with a mic as most people are comfortable with their favourite pair of jeans.

But when it was my turn to be the guest, not the host, something shifted. Before the interview, I was chatting away with the host, relaxed as ever. I felt completely at home, until the mic turned on.

And then... I don't know what happened. I assume it was to do with that magical power of a live microphone that makes you forget your own name. My friend asked me one simple question and suddenly I was overcome with the urge to prove myself. To prove I was smart enough. Credible enough. Good enough.

I'd never been the one answering the questions before. I'd only ever asked them, and apparently, my brain decided the best way to handle this new situation was to firehose the mic with words. Fifteen straight minutes of pure, unfiltered verbal diarrhoea.

Meanwhile, my poor friend was throwing me every SOS signal she had. Tiny inhales to signal she wanted to ask a question, polite raised eyebrows, hand signals, desperate half-smiles. The universal body language for: "Please, for the love of radio, shut up."

And what was my brain doing while all this was happening?

Running an Olympic-level internal monologue:

"Was that good?"
"Did I sound silly?"
"I should say something clever."
"Wait, maybe I should be funny?"
"But not too funny, you need to sound smart too."
"What was the question again? Doesn't matter. Keep talking."

I wasn't connecting. I wasn't even in the room anymore. I was so busy in my head thinking about how to sound good that I forgot to *be* good.

That's when I learned the hard way: if preparation gets you to the interview, mindset gets you through it. If your head's not in the right place, even years of experience can't save you. The real challenge isn't knowing what to say, it's managing your mindset while saying it.

I think three key mindset shifts will set you up for success. Let's set them in your mind.

Self-Talk Yourself Up

Your inner voice can make or break your appearance before you even open your mouth.

Negative self-talk is sneaky. It creeps in with whispers like, "What if I mess up? What if I sound stupid?" And before you know it, you're spiralling before the interview even starts.

Instead of letting doubt run the show, flip the script. Replace *What if I fail?* with *I'm here because I have value to share.*

Psychologist Albert Bandura calls it self-efficacy – the belief that you can succeed when it matters (Bandura, 1997). It's not fluffy pop-psych either: positive self-talk has been shown to significantly boost performance under pressure (Hardy, Hall, and Hardy, 2001). You don't need to be an elite athlete with a mindset coach to make this work. You just need a few simple shifts to put your brain in a better place before stepping up to the mic. Promise.

Try this:
- Write down three positive statements that you say as you walk into every interview – short, positive reminders of why you belong in the conversation. (E.g., "I know my stuff." "People want to hear this." "I'm here because I have something to add.")
- Interrupt negative thoughts with movement – adjust your posture, sit taller, plant your feet, unclench your hands. Even a tiny physical shift can break the loop of self-doubt and snap you back into the moment.
- Refocus on what's already working – instead of worrying about what might go wrong, remind yourself of what's going right. (E.g., "I've prepped for this. I've done interviews before. I know my message.") Read the room rather than your inner-critic.

Don't think of this as faking confidence. It's about choosing a mindset that helps you do the job you've been asked to do. Isn't it time we all stopped the DIY bullying and by actively choosing to self-talk ourself up, rather than down.

Concentrate on Your Expert-Ease

You were invited for a reason — because of what you know, not what you don't. Too often, people panic about the one thing they might not be able to answer, instead of owning what they bring to the table. It might be useful to remember that (most) interviews aren't pop quizzes! You don't need to have all the answers, you just need to know what you already know.

If you get a question you don't know the answer to? Say so, then pivot to your strengths. Audiences don't want perfect anyway. As communication expert Nick Morgan puts it, "Audiences are hungry for authenticity" (Morgan, 2008). People don't want slick. They want real.

Try this:
- Bring it back to what you know. If a question isn't in your wheelhouse, don't force it, steer it toward your expertise instead. Try: "That's a great question, but outside my expertise. What I do know is..."
- Pass the mic. If someone else is better placed to answer, acknowledge their expertise. Try: "I'd love to hear [expert's name]'s thoughts on that. What I can add from my perspective is..."
- Talk about what lights you up from the start. The easiest way to make your message compelling is to talk about what excites you. Passion is contagious.

You don't need to know everything; you just need to own what you do know and share it in a way that feels real and resonates. This is your expert-ese.

Re-Name Your Nerves

Your body doesn't know the difference between nerves and excitement; the only difference is how you label them. Extreme sports athletes don't go searching for anxiety, they go searching for a

When you reframe nerves as energy instead of fear, you can harness them instead of fighting them.

buzz. Base jumpers don't say, "I'm terrified," they say, "I can't wait! Let's go!" It's the same physical reaction, just a different story.

The same principle applies to interviews. Instead of thinking, "I'm nervous," try, "I'm excited." Harvard researcher Alison Wood Brooks ran a study that proved it: when people reframe anxiety as excitement, they perform better, especially when speaking in public (Brooks, 2014). The super cool part is that over time, your brain starts believing you. The more you call it excitement, the less your body treats it like a threat.

So, if your body is already gearing up for action, why not use it to your advantage?

Try this:
- Name it out loud. When nerves hit, don't fight them, relabel them. Take a breath, smile, and say to yourself, "This is just adrenaline. I'm ready."
- Shift your focus outward. Nerves creep in when you're focused on yourself. Instead, think about your audience. How will my message help them? What do they need to hear? Switch your thinking: "How can I help the audience?" instead of "How am I doing?"
- Ground yourself with movement. Adrenaline needs an outlet. Do something with your body to use it up: plant your feet, roll your shoulders, take a sip of water, or stand up and move before the interview starts.

When you reframe nerves as energy instead of fear, you can harness them instead of fighting them. And who knows? If you nail enough interviews, you might even get a shoe named after you... like our next legend.

Learning from Legends: Michael Jordan – Play the Moment, Not the Fear

Even if you don't know much about basketball, you know something about Michael Jordan. His skills were legendary. Interestingly, what made him a game-changer wasn't just about the control he had over a basketball, but also about the control he had over his mind.

Game 6, 1997 NBA Finals – The Ultimate High-Stakes Moment

It's Game 6 of the 1997 NBA Finals — Chicago Bulls vs. Utah Jazz. With seconds left on the clock, the Bulls are trailing by one point. Jordan gets the ball. Instead of freezing under pressure, he takes a deep breath, visualises the ball going through the net, and trusts his training.

He shoots.

He scores.

The Bulls win.

Later, he said, "I never looked at the consequences of missing a big shot… when you think about the consequences, you always think of a negative result." (Lazenby, 2014).

High-stakes moments didn't rattle him. He didn't waste energy worrying about what-ifs. He trusted his preparation, stayed in the moment, and focused on execution, not the fear of failing.

Same goes for interviews.

You don't need to be the GOAT basketballer to do it, you just need to train yourself to show up, trust your prep, and play the game when it counts.

> "People by and large become
> what they think about themselves."
>
> - Bob Rotella, *Golf Is Not a Game of Perfect* (Rotella, 1995)

In-Of-Body Experience – Staying Present and Engaged

After interviewing more than 20,000 people, I've seen this happen over and over again. A guest is mid-interview, and suddenly you can tell they're not fully there anymore.

It happens in two ways:

- Autopilot Mode: their mind starts wandering while their mouth keeps moving. They finish speaking and can't remember what they just said.
- Locked-In Mode: they're so focused on their script that they miss the moment, ignoring key cues, skipping over golden moments, and failing to connect.

Both are obvious. Both are unhelpful. Both are fixable. And both happened to me in the same ten-minute window.

The Fire Alarm Incident

I'd just kicked off a virtual storytelling workshop with 70 people. I was mid-way through my opening story when I noticed someone on screen was waving their hands at the camera. They signalled that no one could hear me. Panic.

I quickly fixed the dodgy tech, restarted my story, and got halfway through again when the fire alarm in my building went off! Seriously?

In those few seconds of alarm-induced chaos, my brain went into overdrive:

"Can they hear the siren?"

"Is this real or a drill?"

"Can I evacuate while staying online?"

"What do I do?"

"Wait… what am I even saying right now?!"

Turns out, while my brain was scrambling for solutions, my mouth was still talking.

I'd gone into autopilot.

Default Mode Network – When Your Brain Takes Over Without You

When the fire alarm went off, it's likely my brain flicked into something called Default Mode Network (DMN), a state where we perform familiar tasks without conscious effort. It's the same thing that happens when you drive somewhere, arrive, and realise you don't remember the trip.

In everyday life, DMN is useful as it frees up brain space for problem-solving, memory consolidation, and creativity. In an interview? It's a disaster. Because when your brain switches to autopilot, you disconnect from the moment. And listeners can tell.

Research shows that when the DMN is active, we're more prone to mind-wandering and less focused on the task at hand (Raichle, 2015). I can always tell when a guest has gone into autopilot; their words keep coming, but their energy drops. Unfortunately, audiences can tell too.

Inattentional Blindness - When You Miss the Gold

But autopilot isn't the only danger. There's another trap – inattentional blindness. Just before the fire alarm, I'd been so focused on delivering my content that it took me a while to notice my audience waving to tell me they couldn't hear me.

Inattentional blindness happens when we're so locked into what we're doing that we miss obvious cues in our environment. A famous study by Simons and Chabris (1999) found that about half of the participants failed to notice a person in a gorilla suit walking through a video they were watching, simply because they were focused on counting basketball passes.

Another study at Western Washington University found that people talking on their phones failed to notice money hanging from trees (Hyman et al., 2010).

That's what happens to guests who get too stuck in their script. They miss real moments to connect, react, and make magic. When you miss the gold, you end up sounding over-rehearsed, robotic, and a little bit... not alive.

To avoid autopilot mode or missing key moments, here are three +1 ways to keep yourself tuned into the moment:

Breathe

Sounds simple. It's not. When nerves take over, our breathing changes first, becoming shallow, fast, and tight.

There's loads of research showing how powerful breathing is, but one of my favourites is from Mark Krasnow from Stanford. He found that deep, steady breathing directly hits the brain's arousal centre, basically switching off panic mode and helping you stay calm and focused (Krasnow, cited in Pyxis Academy, 2023). Turns out, your lungs know how to get you back in the room faster than your brain does.

Try this:
- Notice your breath early. Before nerves take over, check in with yourself. If your breathing is getting shallow, tight, or fast, it's your cue to pause and reset, not power through.
- Try the 4-7-8 breathing technique: inhale for 4 seconds, hold for 7, and exhale for 8.
- Take three deep breaths before speaking. You can also do this during the host's intro or a long question. It's your body reminding your brain, "We've got this."

Over My Dead Body (Language)

Will people know you're nervous? Refer to the title. Yeah, I'm passionate about this one, so let's do the work. Our body speaks long before our words do. In interviews, nervousness leaks out in posture, fidgeting, stiffness, or that deer-in-the-headlights look. While nerves are completely normal, the trick is making sure they don't own the room before you do.

When you take control of your body language, you able to calm yourself and project that calmness (and confidence) to everyone else. In the 1970s, psychology professor Albert Mehrabian figured out something we still haven't fully wrapped our heads around: about 55% of the impression people form of you comes from your body language, not your words (Mehrabian, 1971, cited in Fish Recruit, 2023). Your body can either back you up or throw you under the bus. Do you want it to help or hijack your message?

If you'd prefer the former, instead of letting nerves broadcast themselves, use your body to send a different signal, one that says, "I belong here."

Try this:
- Anchor your feet: plant them flat on the floor. It sounds basic, but it instantly reduces fidgeting and makes you feel more stable. Wobbly legs = wobbly presence.
- Uncross, unclench, un-grip: if you catch yourself folding arms, clenching fists, or death-gripping the table, loosen up. Open posture = open energy.
- Use your hands, but not all at once: let them move naturally when you're emphasising a point. If they start flapping like a semaphore signal, bring them gently back to centre, rest them lightly on your lap or the table between moments.
- Mirror the mood: tune into the host's energy. Are they calm? Curious? Playful? Adjust your posture, expression, or tempo to meet them there. Mirroring helps build connection without saying a word.
- Reset with your breath: if your voice tightens or you start rambling, the above advice works for your body too. Pause and take one slow breath. It softens your shoulders and gives your brain a second to catch up.

If your words say one thing, but your body says, "Help, I'm dying," guess which one people believe?

Put Your Best Face Forward

Ever had someone say, "I'm totally fine!" while their face says, "I'm absolutely not fine"? It's unsettling, right? When we're

In an interview, our face speaks louder than our words. If your expressions don't match your message, people will trust what they see over what they hear. Put simply, your face needs to match your words.

uncomfortable, our facial expressions can betray us. We over-smile, freeze, look horrified, or even seem frustrated. In an interview, our face speaks louder than our words. If your expressions don't match your message, people will trust what they see over what they hear. Put simply, your face needs to match your words.

It takes milliseconds for people to form an impression of you – and, like it or not, your face is doing a lot of the talking (Willis and Todorov, 2006). So, while what you say matters, how you look while saying it matters just as much.

Try this:
- Pause before answering. Give yourself half a second to register the meaning of your words before you speak. This helps your face naturally align with your intent.
- Pre-speech smile. If you're feeling stiff or nervous, smile before you start talking, even a small one. It naturally shifts your energy and helps your voice sound more open and engaging.
- Record yourself in a conversation (not in selfie mode, as you'll get too much visual feedback and change your natural expression). Set up your phone to record while you chat with someone or even while you explain an idea to yourself out loud. Then, watch it back. You'll see how your face moves naturally when you're relaxed versus when you're trying too hard or feeling the pressure.
- Catch your 'nervous face' tells. Do you tighten your jaw? Raise your eyebrows too much? Over-smile? Knowing your go-to nervous expressions means you can work on softening them.

Our audience wants to believe us, so we need to make sure our face isn't accidentally sending mixed messages.

An Extra Tip: Hold a Voice-Warming

I spent the early part of my radio career as a breakfast presenter. This meant my alarm would go off at the highly inappropriate time of 4:20am. I had a five-minute drive to work. I learned very quickly that I needed to spend that time singing loudly to whatever I could. Otherwise, the Penny who was on air at 5:30am sounded very different to the Penny who wrapped up the show at 7:45am.

The first words out of our mouth can set the tone for the whole interview. Yet so many guests cough, croak, or stumble because their voice is still warming up. Voice coach Christina Shewell reckons warming up our voice isn't just for singers and stage actors, it's basic survival for anyone who wants to sound like a human instead of Marge Simpson (Shewell, 2009). Ok, the Marge Simpson reference is mine, but the sentiment is the same. A good warm-up can loosen your jaw, sharpen your articulation, and stop your mouth from tripping over itself when it matters most.

Try this:
- Belt out a song in the car on the way.
- Hum from soft to loud and back again.
- Say 'Benedict Cumberbatch' three times, exaggerating every syllable. What a name!

It feels silly. But better to feel silly before the interview than during it.

> *"Presence is more important than perfection."*
>
> — Amy Cuddy (Presence, 2015)

Before your next interview, commit to:

- Breathing intentionally to keep nerves in check.
- Owning your body language so your presence matches your message.
- Letting your face reflect your words so you don't send mixed signals.
- Warming up your voice so your first words are as strong as your last.

Learning from Legends: Adele – When Being Present Matters More than Being Perfect

There's so much we can learn from Adele about mic dropping moments. While I could take you to almost any interview she's ever done – the honesty, the humour, the heart – I want to take you to a moment that mattered to her. A moment when the stakes were high, the nerves were real, and the whole world was watching.

It's 2017. The Grammys. Adele is on stage, paying tribute to George Michael with a cover of *Fastlove*. A few lines in, she stops. Drops an F-bomb. And asks to start again.

"I'm sorry for swearing and I'm sorry for starting again. I can't mess this up for him," she said, voice cracking, standing there in front of millions of people (Vanity Fair, 2017).

Oh, how I love her! Because right there, in real time, Adele made a choice: not to push through. Not to fake it. But to stay *fully present* and honour the moment.

The audience loved her even more for it. After the performance, speaking backstage, Adele admitted just how much it had weighed on her.

"I did have a shaky rehearsal today," she told reporters. "But I have been working very hard on this tribute for him, every day." (E! Online, 2017). She wasn't trying to be perfect. She was trying to be *real*. To show up properly for herself, for the music, for George and for everyone listening. That's what made the moment unforgettable.

When the pressure's on, focusing on perfection doesn't help. It's about being present with it all — messy bits, F-bombs, and shaky starts.

Lift Your Spirit – How to Bring Authenticity to Every Interview

There are many moments from my ten years on the radio that stand out. But perhaps none were as instantly humbling as a conversation I had two weeks into the job. It was my first-ever 'air check'. It's kind of like a review, where you sit down with your manager and listen back to a recent program. Terrifying for a new presenter.

I remember sitting in the producer's booth, ready to critique my delivery, my pacing, my questions. Before we even hit play, my manager turned to me and said:

"Penny, you need to learn to be yourself on the radio again."

Wait. What? *I am being myself... aren't I?*

Then we listened. And there it was. A 26-year-old me, confidently declaring:

"Well, obviously, when we talk about planning policy in Tasmania, what we know is..."

While imitation can be a
great way to learn,
it's not a way to be.

Except... I knew nothing about planning policy in Tasmania at 26. Still don't. What *was* obvious wasn't the policy; it was that I wasn't being myself. I'd become a master chameleon, imitating other presenters, trying to sound like I thought a radio host should. While imitation can be a great way to learn, it's not a way to be.

A Lesson from a Green House

Determined to figure this out, I went all in. I researched authenticity, I studied myself, and I listened back to my program every day. I learned from the best, took advice from mentors and tried new things. However, the most valuable lesson came, perhaps surprisingly, from a little house I'd pass when I'd walk to work. Yep, from a house, not a person.

It was a typical Tasmanian-looking house; three bedrooms, dusty green weatherboards, with a rusty red corrugated roof. It was on a block that was almost too big, and the lawns were never mowed. It had a short concrete and wrought iron fence with a concrete path leading up to the front door. Alongside that path were the most incredible roses I'd ever seen. They weren't fancy 'standard Icebergs' but big bushy roses of all different heights and colours that seemed to flower all year. They brought colour and chaos and life to this house.

Every time I walked past it, I imagined an older lady must have lived there; she wasn't strong enough to push the lawnmower, but she could look after those roses, and she did it meticulously.

One morning as I walked past, I noticed the tradies had moved in and a renovation had begun. Over the next few weeks, the back block was subdivided off, the short fence became tall, a new roof went on (in Colourbond monument grey), and the dusty green weatherboards became white (my guess is Dulux lexicon quarter... just sayin').

I remember thinking the house looked a million bucks. Then one day I walked past and the roses had been pulled out. They were lying dead on the lawn. It wasn't until that moment of the renovation that I realised the older lady who I imagined lived there must have died or moved on.

And that's when it hit me – what I needed to learn to be *me* when the mic was turned on. Whenever we're speaking in front of an audience, by all means, we can spruce ourselves up and make ourselves look and sound a million bucks, but whatever we do, we can't pull out our roses.

Our roses are our *authenticity markers*. These are the things that make us *us*. Without them, we're just like every other guest on the street, and people will walk past without taking notice (ahem, they won't stop to smell the roses...).

The following three strategies helped me (and continue to help me) get to know and learn to love my 'roses' – my authenticity markers:

- How do others see us – what are the external signals that stick?
- How do others experience our thinking – what is unique about the way we communicate?
- How do we make people feel – what is the emotional imprint we leave behind?

Knowing your roses is the fastest way to 'lift your spirit' so it stands out during interviews and lets your real character shine through.

Wear Yourself on the Outside

First impressions stick whether we like it or not. People form opinions fast, and if we're not intentional about how we show up, they'll fill in the blanks for us.

Most people don't realise that we get a say in how we're remembered. The first step is to make sure the things people see and hear on our outside matches what's on our inside. That way, what people see matches who we are. That's how we help people see the real us quickly and clearly.

It's worth it. Turns out being yourself isn't just nice, it's strategic. In a 2023 study, behavioural scientist Eunsoo Kim and her team put people in high-pressure situations, like job interviews, and found that those who tried to sound impressive were rated as *less* competent and *less* likeable than those who just showed up as themselves (*Kim et al., 2023*).

All that effort to be polished, professional, and perfectly worded backfired. Meanwhile, the people who were authentic – flaws, awkward pauses, and all – built trust faster *and* left a better impression.

So, if you've ever spiralled after an interview thinking, "Ugh, I should've sounded more impressive," the science says... nah. Just be you. Being human beats being polished. Every time.

Try this:
- Wear and Hair: Give them something to remember that is the right fit. It might feel shallow, but people describe us by what we wear, "She was the one in the green jacket with the blonde bob." Clothes, hair, and style help people recall us, so why not make it work for us? Instead of defaulting to some corporate dress code that doesn't feel like you, lean into styles that reflect your personality. It'll boost your

confidence and give you more control over how people describe and remember you.
- Care: What are you always banging on about? When people mention you in conversation, what do they say? "Oh, she's the one who's always talking about storytelling!" The things you care about most are often what make you memorable. So, instead of letting people guess, be intentional about what you stand for. Articulate it clearly and concisely, so people can use it to describe you.
- Flair: Own what makes you *you*. This trumps everything else. What's distinctly, unmistakably you? A signature phrase? Your unexpected hobby? Your deep obsession with a niche topic? Where you live? Lean into it. The more comfortable you are owning your thing, the more people will remember you for it.

So, instead of fitting into an expected template, let's be intentional about showing up as ourselves.

Know What's on Show

People don't just hear what we say, they experience how we say it. Our communication style shapes how others understand our ideas, how they experience our thinking, and whether they care about what we stand for.

There are parts of your style that are totally tweakable – but probably not the ones you think. The habits you feel self-conscious about? They might be the very things that make you memorable. The polished, professional mask you think you need? That might be what's making you forgettable.

When it comes to your communication style, your roses are

Authenticity and adaptability aren't opposites.

the standout traits that make you unmistakably you. These could be your timing, your tone, your curious eyebrow lift, your pause before a punchline, or the way your voice warms when you really care about something. These aren't flaws to sand off. They're petals to protect.

But not every part of your style will suit every situation, and that's okay. Authenticity and adaptability aren't opposites.

Despite what social media might tell us, authenticity isn't about showing up however you feel and expecting everyone to deal with it. It's not "take me or leave me." True authenticity is knowing *who* you are and knowing *where* you are. The skill is in blending the two.

There's a concept in communication research called *bounded authenticity*. In short, people trust you more when you're real, but they trust you faster when you're also responsive to context. Wharton researcher Julianna Pillemer found that people who stay true to themselves and read the room build stronger connections and get taken more seriously (Pillemer, 2025). It's not about faking, it's about filtering, and sometimes, flexing.

I think of it like the *Water Course Way*; a stunning Daoist idea that says water doesn't stop being water when it hits a rock. It shifts. It adapts. Still water. Still doing what it does. But adjusting to where it is to get down the water course successfully. Honestly, I reckon that's a much healthier take on authenticity than "you do you."

This idea connects to what we covered in *Over My Dead Body (Language)*; just as your posture and movement send signals about confidence, your words and tone send signals about who you are and how you connect.

Try this:
- Mannerisms: notice what your body naturally does when you're relaxed. When you're deep in conversation, not performing, not presenting, what's happening? Do your hands move a lot? Do you lean in? Tilt your head when you listen? Raise your eyebrows? Smile in bursts? These little things are part of your style. They're signals people pick up on, often before they even register your words. The goal isn't to fix them. It's just to know them.
- Momentum: notice your natural flow. When you talk, do you build up steam and barrel along? Do you pause and reflect? Do you loop back to ideas or stay on a straight line? Your rhythm, your pacing, your flow, it's all part of how people experience you. No need to force a different style. Just get to know the one you already have.
- Mojo: notice what lights you up. When you're in the groove, what energy are you bringing? Are you witty? Wise? Data-driven? A storyteller? Whatever it is, that's your fire. It's not something you create, it's something you notice and learn how to turn up when you need it.

People don't just hear what we say, they experience how we say it. The more we own our style while staying adaptable, the more compelling we'll be.

Know Your Role

Here's something I've witnessed after 20,000 interviews: people rarely remember your exact word, but they absolutely remember how you made them feel. Of course, it was Maya Angelou who said it best.

> *"People will forget what you said, people will forget what you did, but people will never forget how you made them feel."*
>
> – Maya Angelou

Poetic? Yes. Neuroscientific? Also, yes.

Psychologist Elizabeth Kensinger has spent years studying how emotion affects memory. Her research found that emotionally charged moments don't just pass through the brain, they *etch themselves in*. We remember emotional experiences more vividly and for longer than neutral ones (*Kensinger, 2009*). Basically, if you can create a feeling, you create a memory.

So, if people remember how you made them feel, the next obvious question is: how do you want them to feel?

That's where knowing our role in the moment becomes powerful. Not the formal job title role. Not a role we're always stuck playing. Not a label we carry around. But a *choice*, a strategic decision about how to show up, based on what the moment needs from us and how we want others to experience us.

In my Frequency Thinking™ framework, I talk about four core role archetypes. Four ways of tuning your energy depending on what's needed most.

Here's the short version:

- Anchor: calm and reflective. You steady the moment, slow the pace, and bring grounded presence when things feel shaky or rushed.

- Advocate: clear and perspective-driven. You articulate what others may be feeling or thinking but can't yet say, bringing voice to shared experiences.
- Amplifier: warm and connecting. You lift the energy, spotlight what matters, and help people feel seen, heard, and part of something bigger.
- Adventurer: curious and open. You bring ideas that explore, expand, and uncover new territory, especially when the conversation needs movement or momentum.

We're not locked into one of these roles. We get to choose. And this choice will directly shape the *feeling* we leave behind.

Try this:
- Choose your role: before you speak, ask, *What role would serve this moment best? Anchor? Advocate? Amplifier? Adventurer?*
- Set your intention: decide how you want people to feel when they leave or the interview is over — steady, seen, stirred, supported — and shape your style to match.

Tune your delivery: *focus* on the moment. Switch between these roles as the moment calls for it. You can do them all; it's the switching that gives the conversation texture.

So go on – go and find your roses. Get to know them, learn to love them, then plant them out the front and look after them meticulously. When you nurture what makes you stand out, you'll always be remembered.

Turns out you don't have to be serious to be taken seriously.

Learning from Legends: Annabel Crabb and Leigh Sales – When You Back Your Real Self

If you want proof that showing more of yourself doesn't have to cost you credibility, look no further than Australian journalists and presenters Annabel Crabb and Leigh Sales.

When they launched their podcast *Chat 10 Looks 3*, plenty of people warned them it was a bad idea. In an article in *The Australian*, Leigh talked about how people told her that revealing her love of musical theatre, baking, and books would "ruin her political credibility." That if she let too much of the 'real her' out, she'd lose the serious journalist badge.

Luckily, she didn't listen. Instead of smoothing themselves out to fit some 'serious journalist' mould, they leaned into what made them real. Leigh sharing Broadway recommendations (and often singing them). Annabel sharing kitchen disasters (which are still better than my kitchen wins). Both of them letting their friendship and quirks lead the conversation.

They could turn up on *Chat 10 Looks 3* talking about sourdough starters and show tunes and then turn up on *7.30* or write a hard-hitting political piece, and no one doubted their sharpness or credibility for a second.

That's bounded authenticity in action. Turns out you don't have to be serious to be taken seriously.

The Art and Science of Showing Up and Being Remembered

By now, you've done the prep. You've set the foundations, mapped your message, and run your test. But as you've learned, preparation only gets you to the starting line.

What happens when the mic is on? This is where most guests stumble. They freeze, waffle, overthink, or underdeliver. It's got nothing to do with knowing their stuff and everything to do with knowing themselves.

Not you, though. You've now trained your confidence muscles for the moment. You know how to show up fully, clearly, unmistakably you.

You now know how to:

- Master your mindset so nerves don't hijack your message.
- Have an in-of-body experience so you don't drift into autopilot or miss golden moments.
- Lift your spirit so your authenticity makes you impossible to ignore.

This work keeps you firmly in the right spot or the toast spectrum – not raw, dry, burnt, or slick. You've found the golden zone. Natural. Engaging. Unforgettable.

Now it's time for the final test: what happens after the mic turns off?

Get ready to learn how to turn one moment into ongoing momentum. In the next section, we'll cover how to:

- Leverage every interview to grow your reputation.
- Make sure people don't just hear you, they remember you.
- Grow after every conversation.

After you show up, it's time to focus on the follow up.

After

The Part Nobody Thinks About (But Should)

As previously discussed (in surprising detail), most people treat interviews like a one-night stand. They show up, do their thing, and then disappear, hoping they made an impression but never really knowing for sure.

That's the wrong tactic. The best guests treat interviews more like a long-term relationship. Something worth nurturing, growing, and revisiting. The real magic of a great interview often kicks in after the conversation ends, in the follow-up, the echoes, the opportunities it unlocks. That's where relationships form, reputations build, and resonance happens.

Here's how you do it:
- The Show-Up: turn one conversation into many, so hosts (and audiences) keep calling.
- The Blow-Up: amplify your impact so your message keeps spreading long after the mic turns off.
- The Glow-Up: review, reflect, and refine your performance so every interview is better than the last.

The real magic of a great interview often kicks in after the conversation ends, in the follow-up, the echoes, the opportunities it unlocks.

Guests with that golden toast glow seem to spark momentum. How? Let's get into it.

The Show Up – How to Keep the Conversation Going After the Mic Turns Off

Imagine you've just finished a brilliant podcast interview.

The connection was electric, the conversation flowed effortlessly, and your insights landed perfectly.

What do you do next?

If you're like most people, you:

- Thank the host.
- Get vague details about when it will air.
- Log off or walk out.

And in doing so, you miss the biggest opportunity of the interview!

One afternoon, live on air, a story fell through at the last minute. While this is a very common experience for hosts, the panic was still real. On this particular day, I remember looking directly at my producer, who looked directly at me, and we blurted out the same name simultaneously. Why? Because this person always helped us out. They always had something useful and relevant to say and if they didn't, they knew someone who did. They were generous, reliable, and sharp. The kind of guest we *knew* would deliver.

Every producer, journalist, and host collects these people. Like shells. The perfect ones are hard to find, so when you find them, you keep them. If you think it's the newsworthiness or the expert-ness of your story that makes the biggest impression, soz, you're kidding yourself. Yes, both of those are very important (as I mentioned right at the start of this book), but the relationship trumps them every time. Always. Especially when the pressure's on.

So… how do you become the guest that people collect? The one hosts think of first, call back fast, and recommend freely?

It's about how you *show up* when the mic is *off*. Yes, you need to show up for the recorded conversation, but you also need to show up for the relationship. The best way to do that is to find a way to keep talking with them.

Call Me

Most post-interview conversations end with some variation of *"Thanks for having me"* which is fine. But fine isn't memorable.

If we want to be the guest they think of first, we need to signal that we're open for more. To hark back to the first date metaphor, we need to let them know we are interested and ask them to call.

Try this:
- Be specific about what you can offer next: instead of, "I'd love to come back anytime," try, "If you ever do a follow-up on X, I'd love to dive deeper into that angle – just give me a call." Or, "If you ever need a panel guest on Y, count me in." Or, "I'd love to explore the opposite perspective of what we just covered next time – just give me a call when the time is right."
- Pay attention to what they're working on. If they mention a new project, series, or angle they're exploring, let them know, "That sounds right up my alley, call me if you dive into it. I'd love to contribute."

- Be a source, not just a guest. Let the host know they can call you when they need background, insight, or a quick expert take, even when you're not the featured guest. Try, "If you ever need background on [topic], feel free to reach out. I'm happy to help behind the scenes."

This is all about the reciprocity principle; the idea that when we do something for someone first, they're more likely to want to return the favour.

Psychologists Robert Cialdini (yes, the *Influence* guy) and Noah Goldstein found that people are far more likely to respond positively when you give first, whether it's insight, a quick favour, or just being helpful behind the scenes. It's known as the reciprocity principle. When you offer value upfront, you're laying the groundwork for a stronger relationship later (Goldstein and Cialdini, 2004).

So don't wait for the perfect pitch or polished proposal. Just say something simple in the moment that signals: "Call me. I'm keen. I'm ready. I've got more where that came from." That small offer of value builds trust, shows generosity, and opens the door for what's next.

I'll Call You

You might feel a tendency to follow up just to stay on their radar, however make sure you've got something valuable to share. Something that makes the host's job easier, not harder.

The key is to be seen as a useful resource, not a pest. Make no mistake, hosts can tell the difference. They know when someone is in service to the audience, or when they're just pushing their own agenda. When we show up to genuinely contribute, to support others, share insight, and make useful connections, it builds trust, credibility, and – quietly – influence.

Organisational researchers Flynn, Reagans, Amanatullah, and Ames tracked what happens when people are consistently helpful collaborators. The ones who supported their peers, offered insight, and didn't make it all about them didn't just get thanked, they got noticed. Collected, if you like. Over time, they earned more trust, more status, and more opportunities (*Flynn et al., 2006*).

When you consistently add value, people want you back.

Try this:

- Ask how they prefer to communicate, "What's the best way to keep in touch? Email, LinkedIn, something else?" "Do you have a newsletter or a space where I can keep up with what you're working on?" It shows genuine interest and sets the tone for staying connected.
- Call when you're working on something new. If you've got a project, book, or initiative coming up that's relevant to their audience, let them know. Not as a sales pitch, but as a heads-up, "I'm working on [topic] and thought it might be useful for your listeners. Let me know if it fits!"
- Share when something timely comes up. If there's breaking news or a trending discussion that ties into your expertise, flag it for them. You're helping them stay ahead of the curve, not just pushing for another appearance. Try, "Just saw [topic] come up and it reminded me of our chat. If you're planning coverage, happy to offer a quick take."
- Make it easy. Hosts, journalists, and event organisers are busy. If you can make their life easier, they'll appreciate a call. No one wants an essay in their inbox. Keep your message short, clear, and optional; you're offering, not insisting.

When you consistently add value, people want you back.

By doing this, you stop being just a past guest and start being a trusted resource.

> *"We are drowning in information, while starving for wisdom. The world henceforth will be run by synthesisers — people able to put together the right information at the right time, think critically about it, and make important choices wisely."*
>
> — Edward O. Wilson, *Consilience: The Unity of Knowledge* (1998)

Call My Friend

If you've given all you can, the best way to keep the door open is to open another one for someone else.

This does three things:

- Strengthens your connection with the host. They'll remember that you weren't just looking out for yourself.
- Expands their network with valuable guests. They get more high-quality content.
- Positions you as a go-to resource. Someone they trust to bring in great people.

This is all about social capital; the idea that the more you connect people, the more valuable you become in your network. Sociologist Ronald Burt found that people who act as bridges between otherwise disconnected groups tend to gain more access to information, uncover better opportunities, and hold greater influence within their networks (Burt, 2004). Basically, being a connector isn't just good karma, it's good strategy.

Try this:
- Make it casual, like recommending a great café or local legend. Try, "You know who might be great for your show?" or, "There's someone in my network who's *all over* for this topic."
- Be specific about why they're a great fit. Try, "She's a mental health educator who's brilliant at breaking down tough topics, especially for younger audiences," or, "He's leading this pilot project that ties directly into the theme you're exploring next season."
- Offer the intro, but only if they're keen. Keep it breezy, "Would you be open to an introduction?" or, "Happy to connect you if that's helpful."

Learning from Legends: Oprah Winfrey – The Maya Moment that Never Ended

Would this even be a professional development book without including a story about these two powerhouses?! If you've ever heard Maya Angelou and Oprah Winfrey talk about their friendship, you'll know it didn't start over a wine, a walk, or a crisis involving someone's ex. It started in a TV studio. Lights on. Mic live. Oprah, then a young reporter in Baltimore, was sent to do a short, formal interview with Dr Angelou. It was a standard, run-of-the-mill interview, that would have been insignificant for most guests.

But Maya wasn't most guests. She showed up in service. She wasn't there to hustle a headline. She was there to connect. Importantly, she kept talking after the mic was off because she'd clocked that the woman asking the questions had more to say, too.

Years later, speaking to *Flavorwire* in 2014, Oprah reflected on that first meeting: "We had a short interview, but Maya Angelou never forgot me." When they reconnected in 1984, what began as a five-minute exchange turned into a decades-long friendship, with Maya becoming one of Oprah's most trusted mentors; her "mother-sister-friend," as she's often said.

The post-interview conversations were never about Maya pushing for more screen time. She offered something more valuable: herself. She showed up like the moment mattered, not just to her, but to the person sitting opposite her. That's the kind of guest people remember.

You don't need a platform the size of Oprah's or a voice as iconic as Maya's. You just need to treat the post-interview conversation like it matters. Because it does.

The Best Guests Make Moments Last

Most guests treat interviews like transactions, one and done, onto the next. But the best guests know an interview isn't just a conversation, it's a connection.

They show up after the mic is turned off, making sure the conversation continues.

- "Call me" keeps the door open.
- "I'll call you" keeps the relationship active.
- "Call my friend" expands the network for everyone.

Showing up after the mic turns off helps you turn one interview into momentum.

> *"Givers succeed in a way that creates a ripple effect, enhancing the success of people around them."*
>
> – Adam Grant, *Give and Take*, 2013

The Blow Up – How to Make Your Interviews Impossible to Ignore

I love the idea that where an interview happens isn't where it needs to stay. There are many stories I could share about watching interviews go viral, but I'd rather tell you about something I saw out my back window, 'cause honestly, it makes the same point, but is more interesting.

It started as a casual Saturday morning chat, the kind you forget as soon as you've had your coffee. But by the end of the day, it had turned into something I couldn't stop thinking about.

As I stood watching my then six-year-old play soccer, I got talking to one of the other mums. She mentioned that at 3am, she'd been woken by a call from a friend, urging her to go outside and watch the Aurora Australis – the Southern Lights.

As soon as she said it, I was frustrated. I'd forgotten it was happening. A natural phenomenon, literally in my backyard, and I'd missed it.

Later that evening, as I was doing the washing up and staring out the window into the abyss (as one does when washing up), I noticed something strange. The sky, that should have been dark, was glowing.

Remembering my earlier conversation, I yanked off my washing-up gloves, grabbed my phone, yelled for my husband, and ran outside. And there it was; swirling pinks, purples, and greens dancing across the sky.

But then something even weirder happened. When I looked at the aurora with my naked eye, it was beautiful. Yet when I looked at it through my iPhone camera it was brighter, sharper, and more vibrant than I could see with my own eyes. So, what did I do? I took about a million photos. I then had the very unique thought to post one of these photos on social media. By the time I opened my feed, my social feeds had exploded.

Then the aurora was everywhere; on my phone, my TV, websites, newspapers, Instagram stories (at one point, I had 21 Instagram stories of the aurora in a row).

That's when it hit me: We didn't need to see the aurora to *see* the aurora. Because the people who had seen it, shared it. They amplified it, so even those who weren't outside felt like they had been a part of the moment. That's exactly how you need to think about your interviews.

The Aurora Rule – Visibility Isn't Automatic

A great interview is only half the job. If we want a bigger audience for our interviews, we can't rely on people stumbling across them. We need to take them out of the sky, out of the podcast feed, the magazine, the online article, or the conference stage, and put them where people are looking:

- Their phones.
- Their inboxes.
- Their social feeds.

Yes, people could go and find, and then listen to, the full interview. But will they? Not unless you make it easy for them.

Even if the interview is brilliant, even if it's happening right in their backyard, most people won't remember to go looking for it. Unless we remind them.

Here's how to do it.

Share It

When the interview drops, it's tempting to believe people will find it. But interviews don't spread themselves. We need to help them travel. Just like the aurora, it might be glowing in the sky, but unless someone points it out, most people will miss it.

That's our job. Spotlight it. Share it. Make it easy to find. If you're still cringing at the idea of sharing your stuff, keep this in mind: strategic visibility isn't about vanity, it's about giving. That is what I choose to believe!

Organisational researcher Suzanne de Janasz has spent years exploring why some people rise through the ranks while others, equally capable, stay overlooked. It often comes down to visibility. Not just being *good* at what you do, but making sure the *right people* see it (*de Janasz and Forret, 2008*).

She encourages something she calls strategic self-promotion. The skill of sharing your work where it matters most. The people who do this well make their insights useful, easy to access, and are generous in how they offer value.

In communication terms, that means putting your work where your audience already is. If you've said something worth hearing, make it easy to find.

Don't let it fade into the feed. Light it up. Not for your ego; for your audience.

Try this:

- Make it easy for the host to tag you: provide your social handles and relevant links in advance so they don't have to go hunting mid-post. Make it easy for them.
- Engage with the audience: reply to comments, respond to reactions, and reshare posts. Keep the conversation going.
- Post before your interview goes live: create anticipation so people are already looking for it. Instead of, "Did a great interview today – drops on Friday check it out!" Try, "I had a cracking chat with [Host's Name] about [topic] – we went deep on [key takeaway]. This one drops on [date]."
- Tease, don't dump. Instead of, "New interview! Listen here." Try, "What's the one thing that separates great communicators from average ones? I chatted with [host] on their podcast [name] and we came up with a list. It goes live [date]."

That way, people are already primed to listen when it goes live, and you've done the host a solid!

Shape It

We get to choose how our interview is remembered. Yes, really. We know what was said, but most of our audience doesn't (as they haven't heard/seen/read it yet). We get to pick the frame. We get to decide what stands out. Choose the moments that are most useful or meaningful for your audience and share those. This is something called 'audience-centred messaging', which is a fancy way of saying: make it about them, not you. Roulin and Bangerter (2023) found that content tailored to a specific audience's interests is far more likely to be noticed, shared, and acted on. Yes, it seems like a no-brainer, but most people still post like they're tossing content into the wind. But that wouldn't be you, or would it?

Try this:
- Break it down. Grab a quote, a key idea, a 20-second video, something snackable. Post that.
- Speak to a specific group. Don't say, "Here's my chat on leadership." Say, "Here's what I wish more *first-time managers* knew about leading under pressure."
- Reformat it. Turn audio into a visual quote, turn the quote into a newsletter tip, turn the tip into a reel. Get more mileage from the same moment.

Instead of, "Great chat with [Host's Name] about leadership, have a listen!" Try, "There is one big reason why some leaders can hold a room, while others can't hold a conversation. On [Podcast Name], we talked about the biggest mistake leaders make and how to fix it. Here's my #1 takeaway: [insert takeaway]. You can hear the full episode here: [link]." That way, people know exactly why it's worth their time.

Archive It

Interviews have longer shelf lives than you think. Yet most of us think we can only share things once, and only if we do it straight away. When really, they're less like milk and more like wine! Repurposing content is a well-tread path in digital marketing that we need to follow.

Joe Pulizzi, founder of the *Content Marketing Institute* and one of the original big brains of content strategy, has been saying it for years: the goal isn't to endlessly churn out new stuff, it's to extend

By archiving your best content and resharing it strategically, you're giving it a second (or third or fourth) life. That's bang for your buck. A content bargain.

the life of the good stuff (*Pulizzi, 2014*). His research and work with leading brands shows that creating systems to reshare valuable content, especially when it's tied to a fresh hook or moment, consistently boosts visibility, credibility, and audience trust. We don't always need a brand-new interview. We just need a smart way to bring an old one back, in a way that is relevant.

By archiving your best content and resharing it strategically, you're giving it a second (or third or fourth) life. That's bang for your buck. A content bargain.

Try this:
- Build a library. Create a folder of clips, quotes, and links so you can pull them out when relevant. Make them easy to find.
- Use as proof. Drop links into proposals, pitches, bios, or even create a Spotify playlist to build trust.
- Reshare with purpose. Bring it back when the topic resurfaces in the news, in your work, or in the world.

Instead of, "This interview is a year old, but still relevant!" Try, "A year ago, I spoke to [Host's Name] about [topic] and this insight feels even more relevant today. Here's a clip that still hits home." That way, your old interviews keep working for you.

Learning from Legends: Tiffany Haddish – When the Clip Becomes the Career

When Tiffany Haddish showed up on *Jimmy Kimmel Live!* in 2017 to promote *Girls Trip*, most of the world didn't know her name yet. That changed in under seven minutes.

Instead of doing the usual chit-chat, she launched into a wild story about taking Will and Jada Smith on a Groupon swamp tour. There was a $20 rental car. There were alligators. There was Jada, deeply confused by the concept of Groupon. And there was Tiffany – animated, outrageous, and completely unforgettable.

The audience howled. Kimmel applauded. And the internet lost its mind. The clip got clipped. Then shared. Then re-shared. It was everywhere. More people watched *that* story than the episode itself. And it made her a star.

Groupon saw it too. Within months, she was their new spokesperson. Then she was in their Super Bowl ad. All because of one perfectly told story that lived far beyond the interview. That's The Blow-Up. When you bring a story so good, people want to carry it for you.

Make It Blow Up

- Share It – Get it in front of more people.
- Shape It – Make it matter to *them*.
- Archive It – Keep it working long after it airs.

While we'd like to rely on hope as our strategy for people finding our brilliant interviews it's not enough. By following The Blow up, you're actively ensuring they're impossible to ignore, just like that spectacular aurora in the Tasmanian sky.

The Glow Up – The Reflection Ritual that Changes Everything

Early in my radio career, I built a daily ritual that, in hindsight, fast-tracked my confidence and skills behind the mic.

Every morning, I'd finish my live breakfast show at 7:45am, grab some breakfast, then sit down and listen back to the entire two-hour broadcast from start to finish. Did it take time? Yes. Did other people see the value? Not always. Did it make me significantly better at my job? Absolutely.

At first, I listened back to protect myself from embarrassment. Thousands of people had just heard me live on air, and I needed to know if I'd messed up. Had I said something stupid?

But what I actually learned through the process was much bigger: I had no real sense of how I was doing as I was doing it.

- There was a huge gap between how I thought things had gone and how they actually sounded.
- Moments I thought I nailed? Often, they fell flat.
- Moments I worried I'd stuffed up? They weren't nearly as bad as they felt at the time.

There was so much learning every time I listened back. Turns out, this isn't just a weird overachiever thing – it's a real every person thing. Psychologists call it *reflective practice*. Donald Schön, who literally wrote the book on it, described how progress comes when we pause long enough to notice what surprised or unsettled us, and reflect on what we thought we knew going in. That's when the learning kicks in (Schön, 1983). At the time, I didn't know any of this.

I just knew that when I listened back, I heard things I had completely missed in the moment. Why? Because when we're speaking, our brains are juggling a million things:

- What's my next question?
- Which text message should I read out?
- Am I about to crash into the news bulletin?

My mind was too busy making decisions to fully process how I was coming across. But when I listened back as an audience member, without all the behind-the-scenes distractions, I could finally hear myself objectively and that changed everything.

Early in my career, a much-loved mentor taught me a simple three-step feedback process that makes the whole review process so much easier, so much less-cringe, and so much more useful. Here it is.

What Worked Well?

This is the first question we need to ask when reviewing our work. When I first started listening back, my instinct was to focus on all of my mistakes. I wanted to fix everything. Cut out the fillers, make my phrasing sharper, and stop talking so fast. I'm fairly confident I'm not alone on this.

But I quickly learned that fixing what went wrong is only half the story. Reinforcing what *went right* is just as important… and way more fun (read: less depressing)!

Psychologist Carol Dweck, the brains behind the whole *growth mindset* idea, found that people improve more in the long run when they focus on what's working, not just what's broken (*Dweck, 2006*). Those with a growth mindset don't see weaknesses as permanent flaws, they see them as opportunities to build on what's already strong, to tweak, flex, and grow.

Unfortunately, we're wired to skip over our strengths. We obsess over the fumbles and barely glance at the gold. So, we have to intentionally (force ourselves to) spot what we *did well* – naming it, owning it, repeating it. That's how we build real confidence and consistency.

So yes, review the tape. But don't just cringe at what flopped. Celebrate what flew. Then fly it again.

If we only focus on what we did wrong, we'll start second-guessing ourselves. If we focus on what worked, we can repeat and refine it, making our natural strengths even stronger.

Try this:
- Find three things you did well. Not just fine or acceptable, things that worked. Maybe you told a story that landed, had great pacing, or handled a tricky question with ease. Even the micro moments.
- Find three moments you handled better than you thought. How did those things that felt messy in the moment actually come across? Did you recover well from a curveball? Keep your cool when your brain blanked? Make a solid point even when you felt unsure?
- Write down three things you want to do again. Lock them in. They're the habits that will build your unique voice and confidence. Whether it's the way you opened, a particular phrase that resonated, or a pacing style that felt right.

It's not always about fixing what's broken, but repeating what's working.

What Could Have Been Better?

Listening back to yourself comes with a fair amount of cringe factor. Every weird pause, every awkward phrase, every moment where you *thought* you sounded great but actually sounded like an under-caffeinated version of yourself? Yeah, it's brutal.

The reason it feels cringeworthy is that we take mistakes personally. It's not just, "That moment didn't land," it somehow becomes, "I'm terrible at this."

Science says there's a workaround. Psychologists Ethan Kross and Özlem Ayduk found that when we talk to ourselves in the third person, we take mistakes *way* less personally and learn from them faster (*Kross & Ayduk, 2011*). So instead of spiralling into "I'm the worst," your brain shifts to, "Okay, let's help Penny figure this out" (it wasn't me, it was Penny, and honestly, she's doing her best).

Stepping back like that helps you see yourself the way you'd see a friend or a colleague, with a little more logic and a lot less drama. That's why top athletes watch game footage, not to cringe, but to find patterns and make smart adjustments. Same goes for your playback. Don't listen to beat yourself up, ever, listen to *coach yourself forward*.

Try this:

- Listen like you're reviewing someone else. Imagine you're coaching a colleague – what feedback would you give them? You'd be fair, constructive, and focused on growth.
- Reframe mistakes as data, not failure. Instead of "I was terrible," try, "That didn't land, how can I adjust?"
- Find the patterns. Do you speed up when nervous? Do you waffle when asked a tough question? Do you start strong but trail off at the end?

Reflection without action
is rumination.

Spot the habits and tweak them. The goal is to get better, little by little, every time.

What Will I Do Differently Next Time?

Reflection without action is rumination. And rumination sucks. The real glow-up comes when we turn awareness into adjustment. Once we've identified what worked and what didn't, it's time to plan small, intentional tweaks. James Clear, author of *Atomic Habits*, says that small, repeatable improvements lead to lasting success (Clear, 2018). This makes it feel so much more doable. I'm super sure that you don't need a total overhaul. You need one small improvement per interview.

Try this:
- Identify the trigger: what caused the moment to go off track?
- Choose a new action: what could you do differently next time?
- Recognise the reward: what will improve if you make this tweak?

Example:
- Trigger: I rushed my words during the introduction.
- New Action: Next time, I'll pause and take a breath before speaking.
- Reward: My words will sound clearer, and I'll feel more in control.

If you fix one thing per interview, you'll continuously improve without feeling overwhelmed.

Learning from Legends: Matthew Syed – Hit Play on the Playback

Matthew Syed isn't the kind of guest who wings it and walks away. He's the kind who hits record and then hits rewind. If you don't know him already, Syed's the former Olympic table tennis player turned *Times* columnist and bestselling author of *Black Box Thinking*. He's spent years studying what makes the best... well, the best. What he found is: they review the tape.

Not metaphorically. Literally. When Syed's not writing about high performance, he's living it. He's spoken about how he listens back to his own interviews and speeches to figure out what landed and what got lost. Why? Because the people who keep growing go looking for feedback.

He doesn't sugar-coat it either. In *Black Box Thinking*, he writes:

"Learning from failure has the status of a cliché. But it turns out that, for reasons both prosaic and profound, a failure to learn from mistakes has been one of the single greatest obstacles to human progress."

— Matthew Syed, *Black Box Thinking*, 2015

Translation? If you don't take the time to listen back, you're basically choosing not to get better. Syed treats reflection like an elite sport: you don't just perform, you reflect, tweak, and train for next time. It's about changing the focus from getting things wrong to knowing you can get them *righter*.

So, yes. It might feel cringey. Yes, your voice might sound like it's trapped in a tin can. But if someone who's hosted BBC documentaries, written for *The Times*, and spoken on the world stage still finds value in hitting replay, you probably can too.

Hit play. Hit pause. Hit repeat. That's how you do The Glow Up.

The Conversation That Turns One Moment into Many

You've done the interview. You've delivered, connected, and made an impact and now you know how to go about the critical steps that turn one great conversation into many.

You now know how to complete:

- The Show Up: keeping the conversation alive by staying connected, building relationships, and making sure your name stays top of mind.
- The Blow Up: amplifying your interview so it reaches the right people, in the right way, at the right time.
- The Glow Up: refining your skills by reflecting on what worked, what could be better, and how to make your next interview even stronger.

This is what separates the guests who are one-and-done from those who become go-to voices. They are the stepping stones to:

- New audiences, new collaborations, and new opportunities.
- Becoming someone people don't just hear, but remember, recommend, and call on again.

- Turning a single interview into lasting influence and making sure the message travels further than the mic.

So off you go, go build the habit that makes those things happen. Actually, perhaps finish the book, then build the habit.

Conclusion

You've made it. You've worked through the entire guesting trifecta: Before, During, and After. Not just theory but real, actionable shifts, over three distinct phases. In each phase, we've worked through multiple things to try that will help you move from invisible to influential, irrelevant to resonant, out of obligation and into ownership.

Remember, this isn't just about interviews. These are skills for life. For team meetings. For panels. For moments when you have two minutes to make your point in a packed elevator with a decision-maker and a ticking clock.

Once you start using these tools, you'll notice the ripple effects everywhere:

- Your ideas land clearly in meetings.
- Your presentations feel effortless and natural.
- Your networking conversations turn into real opportunities.
- Your confidence becomes second nature instead of something you have to summon.

I hope you now have a firm sense that being a better guest has got nothing to do with changing who you are, but owning who you are and knowing how to share that in a way that gets you heard, remembered, and invited back.

Then vs. Now

Before you were doing interviews, now you're owning them. Go you. You've moved from winging it to working it. From hoping you did okay to knowing you made an impact. From random results to repeatable success. You don't have to wonder if it's working because you can feel it.

Here's what that shift looks like in action:

BEFORE

The Reccy: From Out of Tune to Aligned

You used to show up out of tune, unaware of (or uninterested in) what the audience needed, and hoping your ideas were amazing enough to just land. You were guessing. But now you've done The Reccy. You've taken the time to tune in before you speak out and you're now aligned with the host and their audience.

The Plan: From Scattered to Settled

Your expertise and ideas used to feel scattered; your ideas, stories, and key points all jumbled in your head. Now you've made the plan. You're settled. You've got structure, but you haven't lost your spark.

The Test Run: From Panicked to Practised

You've done the test run. So instead of panicking about whether the words will come, you feel practised, like they live in your body, not just in your notes.

DURING

Mind: From Edgy to Steady

You used to go in edgy, trying to hit every point but connecting with none. Now you've mastered your mindset and feel steady enough to respond, rather than react.

Body: From Numb to Present

You used to feel numb, as if your face was saying one thing and your thoughts were somewhere else entirely. Now you're in your body, present, bringing the kind of energy that moves with the moment.

Spirit: From Performed to Authentic

You used to sound a little performed, more like a press release than a person. Now you lift your spirit up and out of your script, and you sound authentic, even in the tough bits.

AFTER

The Show Up: From Ghosting to Generous

You used to get ghosted, the interview dropped and that was that. Now you show up afterwards too, staying generous with the host and audience.

The Blow Up: From Self-Serving to In-Service

You used to hold back, reluctant to share beyond the interview, worried it might feel self-serving. Now you know how to make your interviews blow-up to be in service, spreading stories that matter, long after the mic's turned off.

The Glow Up: From Fading to Growing

You used to feel yourself fading, as if the moment passed before you had time to figure out what worked. Now you've built a habit that keeps you growing every time.

Keep Driving

Wherever you are on the road trip from one in a million to the only one, your job now is simple: keep driving.

- If you feel out of tune with the audience, start with **The Reccy**, get curious, not just prepared.
- If your ideas are too loose or all over the shop, revisit **The Plan** and shape them so they actually land.
- If nerves are running the show, go back to **The Test Run** and give yourself a dress rehearsal.
- If you're second-guessing yourself in the moment, return to **Master Your Mindset** and steady the inner chatter.
- If your words are polished but your presence is patchy, find your footing with **In-Of-Body Experience**.
- If you're ticking boxes but not making memories, head to **Lift Your Spirit** and bring some spark.

- If you keep getting crickets after the mic drops, don't disappear, head to **The Show Up** and follow through.
- If your episodes get posted and ghosted, light a match with **The Blow Up** and make your moments travel.
- If you're growing but want to grow faster, track your wins with **The Glow Up** and build your momentum on purpose.

This book isn't a finish line. It's a toolkit. Don't just read it. Use it. Scribble in it. Highlight it. Pass it on to someone who's got big things to say but hasn't quite found their way yet. And remember – great guests aren't born, they're made.

So off you go. Be the guest that everyone wants back.

Once you've done that, I encourage you to flip this book over and get ready to take on the role of the host.

THE END

References

Acunzo, J. (2021, November 26). How to make someone's favourite podcast. *Grow the Show.* https://growtheshow.com/how-to-make-a-podcast-favorite-with-jay-acunzo/

Ali, M. (1975). *The greatest: My own story.* Random House.

Angelou, M. (2009). *Letter to my daughter.* Random House.

Bandura, A. (1997). *Self-efficacy: The exercise of control.* W.H. Freeman.

Beebe, S. A., & Beebe, S. J. (2018). *Public speaking: An audience-centered approach* (10th ed.). Pearson.

Berger, J. (2013). *Contagious: Why things catch on.* Simon & Schuster.

Berne, E. (1964). *Games people play: The psychology of human relationships.* Grove Press.

Brooks, A. W. (2014). Get excited: Reappraising pre-performance anxiety as excitement. *Journal of Experimental Psychology: General, 143*(3), 1144–1158.

Brown, B. (2012). *Daring greatly: How the courage to be vulnerable transforms the way we live, love, parent, and lead.* Gotham Books.

Brown, B. (2020, March 20). *FFTs with Brené Brown* [Audio podcast episode]. In *Unlocking Us*. Spotify.

Burt, R. S. (2004). Structural holes and good ideas. *American Journal of Sociology, 110*(2), 349–399. https://doi.org/10.1086/421787

Church, M., & Cook, P. (2018). *Think: Using Pink Sheets to capture and expand your ideas.* Thought Leaders Publishing.

Cialdini, R. B. (1984). *Influence: The psychology of persuasion.* Harper Business.

Clear, J. (2018). *Atomic habits: An easy & proven way to build good habits & break bad ones.* Penguin.

Cuddy, A. (2015). *Presence: Bringing your boldest self to your biggest challenges.* Little, Brown Spark.

de Janasz, S. C., & Forret, M. L. (2008). Learning the art of networking: A critical skill for enhancing social capital and career success. *Journal of Management Education, 32*(5), 629–650.

Dolan, G. (2017). *Stories for work: The essential guide to business storytelling.* Wiley.

Driskell, J. E., Copper, C., & Moran, A. (1994). Does mental practice enhance performance? *Journal of Applied Psychology, 79*(4), 481–492.

Dweck, C. S. (2006). *Mindset: The new psychology of success.* Random House.

Dziak, M. (2024). Audience analysis. *EBSCO Research Starters.* Retrieved from https://www.ebsco.com/research-starters/communication-and-mass-media/audience-analysis

E! Online. (2017, February 13). Adele reacts to her 2017 Grammy performance redo: "I was devastated." Retrieved from https://www.eonline.com/news/829037/adele-reacts-to-her-2017-grammy-performance-redo-i-was-devastated

Fairhurst, G. T., & Sarr, R. A. (1996). *The art of framing: Managing the language of leadership.* Jossey-Bass.

Ferrazzi, K. (2005). *Never eat alone: And other secrets to success, one relationship at a time.* Currency/Doubleday.

Festinger, L. (1957). *A theory of cognitive dissonance.* Stanford University Press.

Fish Recruit. (2023). The role of body language in first impressions. *Fish Recruit Insights.*

Flavorwire. (2014, May 28). Maya Angelou and Oprah's inspiring public friendship. https://www.flavorwire.com/459582/maya-angelou-and-oprahs-inspiring-public-friendship

Flynn, F. J., Reagans, R. E., Amanatullah, E. T., & Ames, D. R. (2006). Helping one's way to the top: Self-monitors achieve status by helping others and knowing who helps whom. *Journal of Personality and Social Psychology, 91*(6), 1123–1137. https://doi.org/10.1037/0022-3514.91.6.1123

Gallo, C. (2014). *Talk like TED: The 9 public-speaking secrets of the world's top minds.* St. Martin's Press.

Giles, H. (Ed.). (2016). *Communication accommodation theory: Negotiating personal relationships and social identities across contexts.* Cambridge University Press.

Gladwell, M. (2008). *Outliers: The story of success.* Little, Brown and Company.

Glass, I. (2007, March 7). Ira Glass: Tips on storytelling. *Presentation Zen.* https://www.presentationzen.com/presentationzen/2007/03/ira_glasstips_o.html

Goldinger, S. D. (1996). Words and voices: Episodic traces in spoken word identification and recognition memory. *Journal of Experimental Psychology: Learning, Memory, and Cognition, 22*(5), 1166–1183.

Goldstein, N. J., & Cialdini, R. B. (2004). The science of persuasion. *Scientific American, 290*(2), 76–81.

Graen, G. B., & Uhl-Bien, M. (1995). Relationship-based approach to leadership: Development of Leader–Member Exchange (LMX) theory of leadership over 25 years: Applying a multi-level multi-domain perspective. The Leadership Quarterly, 6(2), 219–247.

Grant, A. (2013). *Give and take: Why helping others drives our success*. Viking.

Gross, T. (2018, May 11). Terry Gross and the art of opening up. *The New York Times*.

Hardy, J., Hall, C. R., & Hardy, L. (2001). Quantifying the effects of self-talk on performance. *Journal of Sports Sciences*, 19(12), 865–877.

Hasson, U., Ghazanfar, A. A., Galantucci, B., Garrod, S., & Keysers, C. (2012). Brain-to-brain coupling: A mechanism for creating and sharing a social world. *Trends in Cognitive Sciences*, 16(2), 114–121.

Hayakawa, S. I. (1939). *Language in thought and action*. Harcourt, Brace & World.

Heath, C., & Heath, D. (2007). *Made to stick: Why some ideas survive and others die*. Random House.

Hyman, I. E., Boss, S. M., Wise, B. M., McKenzie, K. E., & Caggiano, J. M. (2010). Did you see the unicycling clown? Inattentional blindness while walking and talking on a cell phone. *Applied Cognitive Psychology*, 24(5), 597–607.

Kensinger, E. A. (2009). Remembering the details: Effects of emotion. *Emotion Review*, 1(2), 99–113.

Kim, T., Seong, J. Y., & Lim, D. H. (2023). Authenticity at work and job performance: The role of trust and work engagement. *Journal of Management*, 49(1), 102–120.

Kross, E., & Ayduk, Ö. (2011). Making meaning out of negative experiences by self-distancing. *Current Directions in Psychological Science*, 20(3), 187–191.

Lawrence, D. (2018, January 31). Tiffany Haddish on why being a Groupon spokesperson beats hanging out with Will Smith. *Entertainment Weekly*. Retrieved from https://ew.com/tv/2018/01/31/tiffany-haddish-interview-groupon-super-bowl/

Lazenby, R. (2014). *Michael Jordan: The life*. Little, Brown and Company.

Locke, E. A., & Latham, G. P. (2002). Building a practically useful theory of goal setting and task motivation: A 35-year odyssey. American Psychologist, 57(9), 705–717.

McCombs, M., & Shaw, D. L. (1972). The agenda-setting function of mass media. *Public Opinion Quarterly*, 36(2), 176–187.

Michie, S., van Stralen, M. M., & West, R. (2011). The behaviour change wheel: A new method for characterising and designing behaviour change interventions. *Implementation Science*, 6(1), 42.

Morgan, N. (2008). *Trust me: Four steps to authenticity and charisma*. Jossey-Bass.

Orji, K., Roulin, N., & Bangerter, A. (2023). Is anybody watching me? Effects of information about evaluators on applicants' use of impression management in asynchronous video interviews. *International Journal of Selection and Assessment*. Advance online publication. https://doi.org/10.1111/ijsa.12515

Petty, R. E., & Cacioppo, J. T. (1986). *Communication and persuasion: Central and peripheral routes to attitude change*. Springer.

Pillemer, J. (2025). The costs and benefits of being your true self at work. Forthcoming publication, Wharton School of Business.

Pink, D. H. (2012). *To sell is human: The surprising truth about moving others*. Riverhead Books.

Pulizzi, J. (2014). *Epic content marketing: How to tell a different story, break through the clutter, and win more customers by marketing less*. McGraw-Hill Education.

Pyxis Academy. (2023). *The science of breathing and focus*. Pyxis Academy Publications.

Raichle, M. E. (2015). The brain's default mode network. *Annual Review of Neuroscience, 38*, 433–447.

Rickards, R. (2000). Planned spontaneity: Managing creative innovation. *International Journal of Technology Management, 20*(5-8), 612–626.

Rotella, B. (1995). *Golf is not a game of perfect*. Simon & Schuster.

Sanfilippo, A. (2023). *Podcasting Made Simple: Strategies to Grow Your Audience and Become a High-Value Guest*.PodPros Media. Obama, M. (2018). *Becoming*. Crown Publishing Group.

Schön, D. A. (1983). *The reflective practitioner: How professionals think in action*. Basic Books.

Shewell, C. (2009). *Voice work: Art and science in changing voices*. Wiley-Blackwell.

Simons, D. J., & Chabris, C. F. (1999). Gorillas in our midst: Sustained inattentional blindness for dynamic events. *Perception, 28*(9), 1059–1074.

So, J., & Song, H. (2023). Two faces of message repetition: Audience favourability as a determinant of the explanatory capacities of processing fluency and message fatigue. *Journal of Communication, 73*(6), 574–586. https://doi.org/10.1093/joc/jqad025

Sweller, J. (1988). Cognitive load during problem solving: Effects on learning. *Cognitive Science, 12*(2), 257–285.

Syed, M. (2015). *Black box thinking: Why most people never learn from their mistakes-but some do*. John Murray.

The Australian. (2018). Leigh Sales and Annabel Crabb: 'There's always something to talk about'. Retrieved from The Australian archive.

Vanity Fair. (2017, February 12). Adele's George Michael tribute at the Grammys: Watch her start over mid-performance. Retrieved from https://www.vanityfair.com/hollywood/2017/02/adele-george-michael-grammys-2017-tribute-start-over

Waller-Bridge, P. (2019, April 8). The Tonight Show Starring Jimmy Fallon [TV broadcast]. NBC.

Waller-Bridge, P. (2019, March 8). Woman's Hour [Radio broadcast]. BBC Radio 4. Quoted in Burton, N. (2019, March 8). Phoebe Waller-Bridge reveals Fleabag's origin story. *Mashable.* https://mashable.com/article/phoebe-waller-bridge-fleabag-inspiration

Watts, A. (1975). *Tao: The watercourse way.* Pantheon Books.

Whyte, D. (n.d.). Life at the frontier: The conversational nature of reality [Lecture]. Many Rivers Press.

Willis, J., & Todorov, A. (2006). First impressions: Making up your mind after a 100-ms exposure to a face. *Psychological Science, 17*(7), 592–598.

Wilson, E. O. (1998). *Consilience: The unity of knowledge.* Alfred A. Knopf.

Yahr, E. (2017, July 24). Tiffany Haddish and the magic of one hilarious story on late-night TV. *The Washington Post.* Retrieved from https://www.washingtonpost.com/news/arts-and-entertainment/wp/2017/07/24/tiffany-haddish-and-the-magic-of-one-hilarious-story-on-late-night-tv/

Yates, F. A. (1966). *The art of memory.* University of Chicago Press.

Acknowledgements

Writing this book wouldn't have been possible without the belief, encouragement, and ongoing support of so many people around me. While writing can look like a solitary act, it's held up by many hands.

To my sister and business partner, Lucy Byrne – thank you for always being my fiercest champion, my sounding board, and the one who reminds me that my biggest ideas are worth chasing. I'm not sure the first pages of this book would ever have been written without you in my corner! To Ange Argyle, my business manager – thank you for making space for me to write, for holding the details I so easily drop, and for keeping the wheels turning.

To my husband Barney, and to my children Banjo and Vinny – thank you for trusting me completely, for cheering me on, for sharing the stories I learn from, for making me laugh when I most need it, and for bringing me dinner when I'm still typing late into the night. You remind me every day why this work matters.

To my dad, brother, and band of legendary in-laws and friends – thank you for your unwavering interest in my work and for never doubting that I can do what I say I can, even when the evidence isn't yet there. Your belief is huge, and it holds me steady.

I am endlessly grateful to the generous circle of pre-readers and thought leaders who gave their time, honesty, and belief. You are forever my mentors, perspective checkers, and reality keepers. Your feedback and encouragement shaped these words in ways that will never be visible on the page, but will be felt in every conversation this book sparks.

Finally, to all those who remind me, through both their patience and their challenge, that storytelling is never finished - thank you.

Wood, W., Quinn, J. M., & Kashy, D. A. (2002). Habits in everyday life: Thought, emotion, and action. *Journal of Personality and Social Psychology, 83*(6), 1281–1297. https://doi.org/10.1037/0022-3514.83.6.1281

Yumi Stynes - Me and Alcohol Don't Mix [Video]. (2024, June 9). YouTube. https://www.youtube.com/watch?v=OHDMoSA23ao

Zak, P. J. (2011). *The moral molecule: The source of love and prosperity*. Dutton.

Sinek, S. (2009). *Start with why: How great leaders inspire everyone to take action*. Portfolio.

Slamecka, N. J., & Graf, P. (1978). The generation effect: Delineation of a phenomenon. *Journal of Experimental Psychology: Human Learning and Memory, 4*(6), 592–604. https://doi.org/10.1037/0278-7393.4.6.592

Smith, L. H., Patel, R., & Nguyen, T. (2024). Trust me: How consent-based content sharing boosts audience engagement and credibility. *Journal of Communication and Media Ethics, 31*(2), 144–160.

Spiro, R. J., & Jehng, J. C. (1990). Cognitive flexibility and hypertext: Theory and technology for the nonlinear and multidimensional traversal of complex subject matter. In D. Nix & R. Spiro (Eds.), *Cognition, education, and multimedia: Exploring ideas in high technology* (pp. 163–205). Lawrence Erlbaum Associates.

Stynes, Y. (2022, September 10). Life is long w/ Yumi Stynes [Audio podcast episode]. In *Multi-Hypho* (Ep 9). Candy Bowers. https://candybowers.com/multi-hypho-podcast/life-is-long-w/-yumi-stynes

Sweller, J. (1988). Cognitive load during problem solving: Effects on learning. *Cognitive Science, 12*(2), 257–285.

The Daily Show with Trevor Noah. (2022, December 8). Final episode [Television broadcast]. Comedy Central.

The Design Files. (2018, July 18). Yumi Stynes talks parenting, her podcast, cookbook, and more. https://thedesignfiles.net/2018/07/yumi-stynes-family

The Oprah Winfrey Show. (2010–2011). Season 25 [Television broadcast]. Harpo Productions.

Wood, C. (2019, November 7). *Finding new ways to grow old* (S. Kanowski, Interviewer) [Audio podcast episode]. In *Conversations*. Australian Broadcasting Corporation.

McSpadden, K. (2015, May 14). You now have a shorter attention span than a goldfish. *TIME*.

Mehrabian, A., & Russell, J. A. (1974). *An approach to environmental psychology*. MIT Press.

Murdock, B. B. (1962). The serial position effect of free recall. *Journal of Experimental Psychology, 64*(5), 482–488.

Newton, E. L. (1990). The rocky road from actions to intentions (Doctoral dissertation). Stanford University.

Nielsen Norman Group. (2023). The funnel technique: A method for structuring questions. https://www.nngroup.com

Perkins, M. (2021, September 15). Canva's $40b valuation: 'We got 100 no's before a single yes'. *The Australian Financial Review*. https://www.afr.com/technology/canva-s-40b-valuation-we-got-100-no-s-before-a-single-yes-20210915-p58ryu

Press Club Institute. (2020, November 19). The Art & Craft of the Interview: How to Deeply Listen [Webinar]. https://www.pressclubinstitute.org/

Rogers, C. R. (1957). *The necessary and sufficient conditions of therapeutic personality change*. Journal of Consulting Psychology, 21(2), 95–103. https://doi.org/10.1037/h0045357

Russell, A. (2025, January 3). Graham Norton would like a chat. *The New Yorker*. https://www.newyorker.com/culture/drinks-with-the-new-yorker/graham-norton-would-like-a-chat

Sales, L. (2022). *Storytellers: Questions, answers and the craft of journalism*. Simon & Schuster Australia.

Sales, L., & Crabb, A. (2017, December 15). Episode 72: End of another year [Audio podcast episode]. In *Chat 10 Looks 3*. https://www.chat10looks3.com/podcast/ep72

Schön, D. A. (1983). *The reflective practitioner: How professionals think in action*. Basic Books.

Glass, I. (2018, May 17). Ira Glass's commencement speech at the Columbia Journalism School graduation. *This American Life.* https://www.thisamericanlife.org/about/announcements/ira-glass-commencement-speech

Goldsmith, M. (2003). *What got you here won't get you there: How successful people become even more successful.* Hyperion.

Goleman, D. (2006). *Social intelligence: The new science of human relationships.* Bantam Books.

Gross, T. (2012, May 8). Fresh Air Remembers Maurice Sendak. NPR. https://www.npr.org/2012/05/08/152248901/fresh-air-remembers-childrens-author-maurice-sendak

Gross, T. (2015, January 4). Terry Gross and the art of opening up. *The New York Times Magazine.* https://www.nytimes.com/2015/01/04/magazine/terry-gross-and-the-art-of-opening-up.html

Hamish & Andy. (2024). *Hamish & Andy* [Podcast]. LiSTNR.

Hamish & Andy. (2024). *Remembering Project* [Podcast]. LiSTNR.

Hari, J. (2022). *Stolen focus: Why you can't pay attention and how to think deeply again.* Bloomsbury Publishing.

Häfner, S., Stock, A., & Oberst, V. (2014). Avoiding procrastination through time management: An experimental intervention study. *Educational Studies, 40*(3), 352–360. https://doi.org/10.1080/03055698.2014.899487

Johnson, A. M., & Smith, K. L. (2023). The network ask: How direct requests boost reach, reciprocity, and response rates in digital communication. *Journal of Social Media and Network Science, 12*(1), 58–74.

Kahneman, D., Fredrickson, B. L., Schreiber, C. A., & Redelmeier, D. A. (1993). When more pain is preferred to less: Adding a better end. *Psychological Science, 4*(6), 401–405.

Deimen, M., & Szalay, D. (2019). Expert communication challenges.

Edmondson, A. (1999). *Psychological safety and learning behaviour in work teams.* Administrative Science Quarterly, 44(2), 350–383. https://doi.org/10.2307/2666999

Emmons, R. A., & McCullough, M. E. (2003). Counting blessings versus burdens: An experimental investigation of gratitude and subjective well-being in daily life. *Journal of Personality and Social Psychology, 84*(2), 377–389.

Ericsson, K. A., Krampe, R. T., & Tesch-Römer, C. (1993). The role of deliberate practice in the acquisition of expert performance. *Psychological Review, 100*(3), 363–406.

Feldman, J. M., & Lynch, J. G. (1988). Self-generated validity and other effects of measurement on belief, attitude, intention, and behaviour. *Journal of Applied Psychology, 73*(3), 421–435. https://doi.org/10.1037/0021-9010.73.3.421

Fennell, M. (2021, November 12). Stuff The British Stole's Marc Fennell: 'I think a lot of white Australia has never really thought about it'. *The Sydney Morning Herald.*

Friedman, H. S., & Riggio, R. E. (1982). Nonverbal skills and status attainment among males. *Journal of Nonverbal Behaviour, 6*(3), 178–192. https://doi.org/10.1007/BF00987257

Gallo, C. (2014). *Talk like TED: The 9 public-speaking secrets of the world's top minds.* St. Martin's Press.

Game On! Podcast Episode #14 – Jennifer Gonzalez from Cult of Pedagogy. (2024, August 12). https://resources.breakoutedu.com/blog/gameonpodcast-cult-of-pedagogy

Gino, F., Staats, B. R., & Staats, E. B. (2015). The microstructure of work: How job tasks affect effort and performance. *Harvard Business School Working Paper,* No. 15-009.

Brown, M., Richards, H., & Tan, J. (2023). The impact of post-event reflection on memory consolidation and emotional resonance. University of Queensland, Department of Psychology. [Preprint].

Cain, S. (2022, January 21). Ira Glass: 'I'm not a natural storyteller'. *The Guardian*.

Chartrand, T. L., & Bargh, J. A. (1999). *The chameleon effect: The perception–behaviour link and social interaction*. Journal of Personality and Social Psychology, 76(6), 893–910. https://doi.org/10.1037/0022-3514.76.6.893

Chartrand, T. L., & Bargh, J. A. (1999). The chameleon effect: The perception–behaviour link and social interaction. *Journal of Personality and Social Psychology*, 76(6), 893–910. https://doi.org/10.1037/0022-3514.76.6.893

Chesebro, J. L., & McCroskey, J. C. (2001). The relationship of teacher clarity and immediacy with student state receiver apprehension, affect, and cognitive learning. *Communication Education*, 50(1), 59–68.

Clear, J. (2018). *Atomic habits: An easy & proven way to build good habits & break bad ones*. Avery.

Columbia Journalism Review. (2015, August 13). Interview with Terry Gross. https://www.cjr.org/q_and_a/terry_gross_interview_npr_fresh_air.php

Cuddy, A. (2015). *Presence: Bringing your boldest self to your biggest challenges*. Little, Brown Spark.

Cuddy, A., Kohut, M., & Neffinger, J. (2013). Connect, then lead. *Harvard Business Review*, 91(7), 54–61. https://hbr.org/2013/07/connect-then-lead

Cult of Pedagogy [@cultofpedagogy]. (2024). Posts [Twitter profile]. X. https://x.com/cultofpedagogy?lang=en

Cult of Pedagogy Podcast. (2024). Hosted by Jennifer Gonzalez. https://www.cultofpedagogy.com/pod/

References

ABC. (2024). *Conversations with Sarah Kanowski* [Radio broadcast]. ABC Radio.

ABC News. (2022, June 30). *Farewell to Leigh Sales: A 7.30 Special* [Television broadcast]. Australian Broadcasting Corporation. https://www.youtube.com/watch?v=TdOYN01cc5w

ABC Radio National. (n.d.). *Stop Everything!* https://www.abc.net.au/radionational/programs/stop-everything/

Angelou, M. (2009). *Letter to my daughter*. Random House.

Attenborough, D. (2020). *The secret world of bats* [Video]. Smithsonian Channel. https://www.youtube.com/watch?v=qJOloliWvB8

Australian Financial Review. (2023, March 8). Melanie Perkins: The power of persistence. https://www.afr.com/work-and-careers/leaders/melanie-perkins-the-power-of-persistence-20230308-p5cqk2

Bodie, G. D., Veksler, A. E., & Cannava, K. (2015). The role of active listening in informal helping conversations: Implications for communication training. *International Journal of Listening, 29*(3), 134–149.

- If you're still guessing what people need, go back to **The Calibration** and bring the audience with you.
- If you're drowning in ideas, return to **The Curation** and filter for what matters most.
- If you're rushing in and hoping for the best, revisit **The Preparation** and get in tune before the mic goes live.
- If you feel scattered come showtime, head to **The Rituals** and be intentional about a repeatable rhythm.
- If connection feels patchy, check back in with **The Rapport Card** and get better at tuning in to their frequency.
- If your questions are landing flat, grab **The Route** and steer the conversation like it's going somewhere.
- If the moment fizzles too fast, start with **The Share** and shape how it's remembered.
- If nothing's coming from your best work, use **The Art of Asking** and throw out some stones.
- If you're plateauing, go to **In Reflection** and build rituals that make you stronger every time.

This book isn't your grand finale. It's your how-to guide. Highlight it. Mark it up. Dog-ear the pages and pass it to someone who doesn't know that great hosting is learnable.

Now off you go.

Be the host who shapes the conversation... and in doing so, shapes the culture of your community.

THE END

Conclusion

highlight what mattered, offer real gratitude, and extend the impact generously, deliberately, and with care.

The Art of Asking: From Assuming to Asking

You used to wait, hoping for feedback, assuming people would share, refer, or return on their own. Now you know better. You ask. You check for permission. You ask what stuck. You ask for the next conversation. And you do it in a way that builds trust, momentum, and genuine connection every time.

In Reflection: From Critical to Curious

You used to repeat the same patterns, sometimes without even realising it. When things went wrong, you were more likely to cringe than to learn. Now you reflect with curiosity. You spot what worked, notice what didn't, and explore why. You adjust, test, and embed what's useful, turning every moment into something you can build on.

Why? Because you've built the right instincts and packed the right tools.

Great hosting isn't just one skill. It's a stack of skills working together before, during, and after every conversation.

When you balance it all? You stop thinking about hosting.

You just host.

Keep Hosting

No matter how full your toolkit is or how ingrained your instincts have become, the shift from making it up to making it matter doesn't end here. Your job now is simple: keep hosting.

No matter how full your toolkit is or how ingrained your instincts have become, the shift from making it up to making it matter doesn't end here. Your job now is simple: keep hosting.

DURING

Rituals: From Default to Intentional

You used to fall into default mode, winging it, rushing it, or clinging to a script just to feel steady. Now you use rituals to anchor you. You start with intention. You know how to centre yourself before stepping in, so you show up focused, not flustered. Grounded, not grasping. Ready, not rattled.

Rapport: From Clunky to Connected

You used to feel clunky trying to build trust, unsure how to warm things up, mirror the energy, or make your guest feel safe to share. Now you build rapport with purpose. You find common ground quickly. You tune in to tone, match pace, and create the kind of connection that helps people open up and lean in.

Route: From Drifting to Navigating

You used to either stick to the script or drift between questions, unsure how to pivot when things changed or when a surprising moment showed up. Now you navigate with confidence. Using The Question Compass, you've got tools to help you focus on outcomes to find the answers you need and instincts to help you read the conversation and shift when needed. You don't just feel your way through the conversation; you guide it, deliberately.

AFTER

The Share: From Shallow to Generous

You used to shut the laptop, turn off the mic, and move on. The moment passed, and that was that. Now you know that how you share afterwards shapes how the moment is remembered. You

Then vs. Now

Let's look at what's shifted.

BEFORE

Calibration: From Guessing to Aligning

You used to go in guessing, hoping that the tone was right, the guest was ready, and the audience would care. But these three moving parts were often out of sync. You could feel it... you just didn't know what it was, or how to fix it. Now you calibrate. You tune yourself, your guest, and your audience toward the same purpose. You're not guessing, you're *aligning*.

Curation: From Cluttered to Clear

You used to arrive *cluttered*, with too many half-baked ideas, and not enough filter. It felt scattered, rushed, a little bit of everything but not quite enough of anything. Now you curate. You're *clear* on what's worth including and what's better left behind. You know the difference between interesting and easy, and you build from there.

Preparation: From Static to Resonance

You used to prepare by scrambling, if you prepared at all. You'd go in focused on that content, but not conditions. The result? *Static*. Mismatched energy, missed cues, and a moment that never quite landed. Now you prepare for *resonance*. You go beyond the script and prepare the space, nurture the relationships, and are aware of the energy you're walking into and want to leave behind.

Conclusion

You did it. You've worked through every phase – Before, During, and After – and unpacked what it really takes to be a better host. A host who does more than show up and steer, but one who shapes the space, sets the pace, and builds resonance that lasts.

You've added rituals, reflections, questions, and habits. You've learned how to prepare, listen, pause, shift, and follow up like someone who knows what they're doing, because now, you do.

Hosting isn't magic. It's not luck. It's not a personality type. It's a craft. A craft known to Orienteering Bats and the makers of Golden Toast. This book has shown you how to hone it. You've now got multiple things to try, in each of the three distinct phases.

While this book talked about podcasts, panels, meetings, and events, really, it's about conversations. It's about leadership. It's about how you show up when it counts.

When most people turn up as a host, they're simply hoping it goes well. Now you can turn up knowing *how* to make it go well.

Let's take a breath. Look back one last time. And see how far you've come.

What Happens After Is What Makes You Better

You've done the gig. You prepped like a pro, hosted like a human, and shared like someone who actually cares. And now you know not to switch off and vanish. You know that it's time to squeeze the juice. Build momentum. Make it count.

Here's what you've added to your toolkit:

- You share with purpose, offering real gratitude, thoughtful feedback, and choosing what sticks in people's minds long after the moment ends.
- You ask with guts, getting permission, planting seeds, and keeping the ripples moving well beyond the mic drop.
- You reflect with intent, spotting what worked, adjusting what didn't, and folding those lessons into your flow so they show up next time without effort.

These steps are the difference between hosts that plateau and those that keep getting better.

So, go on. Send the thank you. Make the ask. Do the cringeworthy play-back. It's what you do after is what makes you unforgettable.

That's exactly what the best hosts do. Not just in front of the mic, but behind the scenes. They replay, review, refine, and embed. Not to self-flagellate, but to get better for next time.

If this book's taught you anything by now, (surely) it's this: hosting doesn't end when the event does. Some of the best stuff happens after. That's where clarity lives. Where growth takes root. Where you figure out what worked, what didn't, and what you'll carry forward.

So, the next time something lands flat, or soars, pause. Debrief. Choose one thing to tinker with. Then get back in the chair. It doesn't have to be flashy. It just has to be deliberate. Even though reflection comes after the event, treat it more like a rehearsal than an encore.

The Best Hosts Keep Learning

I'm sure you're all over it now – the biggest impacts often happen after you've hosted.

By taking the time to reflect, you:

- Review with curiosity. Notice what worked, what didn't, and what genuinely surprised you, without judgment.
- Make small, intentional improvements. Tweak one thing at a time, gradually refining your craft with each conversation.
- Embed what works into your rituals. Don't leave the good stuff to chance, make sure it becomes part of how you show up, every time.

You don't have to get it perfect every time, but you do need to get better every time.

Learning from Legends: Melanie Perkins – Growth Starts After

We've already heard from a celebrity host in this section, so let's switch the script and turn to the business world. To someone who's built one of the world's most successful platforms without ever pretending to have it all sorted: Melanie Perkins, co-founder and CEO of Canva, is a powerhouse (obvs) and world-class reflector.

If you don't know her story, here's the nutshell version: Melanie started pitching the idea for Canva while she was still at uni in Perth, Australia. She and her co-founders hit up investors around the world and copped "no" after "no" after "thanks-but-no" in Silicon Valley. Heaps of rejections. But instead of folding, they turned each one into a kind of post-match review. What landed? What didn't? What's the next small tweak?

They weren't sitting around waiting for a breakthrough or using magical thinking, they worked for it by building reflection into their process. They'd sharpen the story, tweak the deck, clarify the vision, then fly across the globe to try again. And again. And again (Perkins, 2021; *AFR*, 2023).

That's the bit I love. It wasn't one grand reinvention. It was a thousand small shifts, stacked over time. Melanie didn't overhaul everything after every rejection; she just chose the next thing to improve. A better story here. A clearer goal there. And over time, those tweaks turned Canva into a global giant (that I would be lost without).

But what makes her legendary — at least in my book — is that this reflection wasn't a one-off. It became a rhythm. A built-in ritual. She's said, "Every time we got a 'no,' we'd ask ourselves, 'What can we learn from this? How do we get better for the next one?'" (Perkins, 2021).

we don't improve by force of willpower, we improve by creating systems that make the right actions easier to repeat (Wood et al., 2002). If you have to remember to do it from scratch every time, you won't. But if it's baked into your process? You're golden.

This is how rituals are born. We discussed this back in *The Rituals* section. But what I didn't say then is that many of the best rituals aren't designed in advance. They're discovered in reflection. Refined. Embedded. Bit by bit. So that the little moment you repeated once or twice becomes your go-to. Your rhythm. Your magic.

The goal here is to turn insights into instincts. To hardwire what's working, so you don't have to think so hard next time.

Try this:

Turn your best learnings into rituals:

- Did that format of that new opening question nail the tone? Great. Add it to your prep template so you don't forget it when the pressure is on.
- Did a last-minute mic check save your butt? Excellent. Make it part of your non-negotiables. Pop it into your tech checklist right now.
- Did sending a thank-you message create a brilliant follow-up moment? Beautiful. Set a recurring calendar reminder to send a text ten minutes post-gig.
- Did pausing more improve the pace and feel? Magic. Add it to your sticky-note stack. One word will do: *BREATHE*. Stick it where you'll see it (maybe just beside your laptop camera lens).

Just as you can create rituals to make the good stuff stick, you can also change your rituals to let the bad stuff go.

- Maybe it's pausing a beat longer before you ask the next question. Give your guest space to think and yourself space to listen. That beat might be where the gold lives.
- Maybe it's inviting more reflection from your guest. Go beyond what happened. Ask what it meant. That's often where the insight sits.
- Maybe it's reining in the rambles (yours or theirs). Notice when the conversation drifts too far off course. Practise gently steering it back with clarity *and* care.
- Maybe it's warming up your voice so you don't sound like a lawnmower in winter (we've all been there). Even two minutes of humming, stretching, or talking to yourself like a weirdo can help you start stronger.

Then test it. Notice what changes. And when it works? Lock it in. Improvement isn't about constant change. It's about intentional evolution.

Embed It

You've done the hard bit. You reflected. You refined. You found the thing that made everything smoother, sharper, stronger. Now don't lose it.

One of the biggest mistakes hosts make is treating improvement like a one-off. They do something that works and then forget to do it again. Guilty. You might say it's like finally learning how to make perfect toast... and then going back to burning it because you didn't write down the settings.

Embedding isn't about getting rigid. It's about making the good stuff repeatable. The idea comes straight from habit formation research. Behavioural scientists like Wendy Wood have shown that

The best hosts don't reinvent the wheel after every chat. They tighten a spoke. Shift the weight. Add a little air. It's the difference between being reactive and being deliberate.

Improve it

Okay, so you've cringed your way through the playback. You've done the reflection. You've spotted the moment where the energy dipped, or your question landed sideways, or you said "um" 17 times in two sentences. Now what?

The trick is not to try to fix everything at once. The best hosts don't reinvent the wheel after every chat. They tighten a spoke. Shift the weight. Add a little air. It's the difference between being reactive and being deliberate.

Psychologist K. Anders Ericsson spent decades studying what makes experts different from everyone else. Spoiler: it's not natural talent. It's deliberate practice, the kind of focused, structured improvement where you isolate one thing, work on it, test it, and repeat.

"Expert performance is not attained by the mere repetition of a task, but by deliberate efforts to improve."

– K. Anders Ericsson, Ralf Th. Krampe, and Clemens Tesch-Römer, *The Role of Deliberate Practice in the Acquisition of Expert Performance* (1993)

So no, you don't need to overhaul your voice, your format, your life. You just need to adjust one dial at a time until the (toaster) settings are just right.

Try this:

After every hosting gig, pick one thing to improve next time. Just one.

Which brings us to Donald Schön, the reflective practice guy. He spent his whole career studying how professionals improve. He found we don't grow just by doing the thing. We grow by *thinking* about how we do the thing. He called it "reflection-in-action" (Schön, 1983). It's what turns automatic habits into intentional craft.

Rather than thinking about reflection as cringeworthy, think of it as part of the craft.

Try this:

- Find a way to record the moment. If it's literally recorded, great, you can listen or watch it back. If it wasn't, jot down a few quick voice notes or reflections while it's still fresh. Capture what you can before it vanishes into the blur of what's next.
- Review it and learn. Cringe is part of the process. But so is clarity. Re-listening helps you hear what really happened, not just what you remember happening. To make it easier, pretend the person you're listening to or watching is someone else and you're simply providing them with some useful notes!
- Ask yourself: what clicked? What dragged? Note the standout moments and the flat ones. Where did the energy shift? Where did you lose flow?
- Dig into why something didn't work. Don't stop at "that bit felt off." Be specific. Was it the pacing? The question? The framing? Capture the mechanics, not just the mood.

What you hear and see when you review your efforts will teach you more than any course, script, checklist, or – ahem – book. Even if you need to watch through your fingers the first few times.

Cringe is part of the process. But so is clarity. Re-listening helps you hear what really happened, not just what you remember happening.

everything and was this totally empowered woman," she says, "but I've still so much to learn. I feel different, I am different, because of this podcast" (Stynes, 2022; *The Design Files*, 2018).

She doesn't rush that process either. She's described it as "tinkering away" – redrafting, adjusting, sitting with something (Stynes, 2024).

That's reflection at its best. Not a full-scale reinvention. Just slow, thoughtful, honest improvement.

So, as we step into this final phase of hosting brilliance — reflection — don't think of it as the wind-down. It's the bit that makes everything else stronger. It's where you notice what you can't hear when you're 'in it'.

Maybe it's perfect that Yumi's only showing up now, in the part that really makes the difference in becoming a better host, yet most avoid.

Don't avoid it. Do it well.

Review It

Whenever I suggest clients should listen back to their own interviews or presentations, I get the same reaction. A full-body cringe. You're picturing it now and you know the feeling that comes with it. People will do almost anything to avoid watching or listening to themselves back. Clean the fridge, organise receipts, get into crypto. Anything. I get it. I've been there.

Back in my early ABC days, I listened back to every single show. Not because I loved the sound of my own voice (I didn't), but because it was the only way to hear what I couldn't hear in the moment. The stumble I didn't notice. The moment I missed. The question I nailed without realising. Listening back let me *tune in*, to me.

In Reflection – The Final Three Steps to Hosting Brilliance

I am a big reflector. Not because I'm naturally still or introspective (far from it), but because I've learned that's where the real shifts happen. In the space *after* the spotlight. The work between the work.

So, you can imagine how excited I was to discover that one of my favourite hosts is a big reflector, too. The weird thing is, I almost didn't include her in this book. Well, I did, in early drafts; she popped up everywhere. I had to keep deleting her so she didn't steal the whole book. But somehow, I've ended up here, at the very end, and am only now bringing her in. Which feels... wrong. And also, exactly right.

Because Yumi Stynes is the kind of host you talk about after, when you're unpacking what made something work. Yumi is the host of podcasts *SEEN* and *Ladies, We Need to Talk*. She has been a TV presenter on *Channel V Australia*, *MAX*, and *The Circle*. She's done radio, written books, and had many controversial moments. I love listening to the way she 'is' with guests, giving them plenty of room and acknowledgement, and how her warmth and wit bring her curiosity out. But it's her awareness that really gets me. The way she listens. The way she lets conversations breathe. The way she pays attention after the interview as much as during it.

What I didn't know until I dug deeper is that Yumi's career as a host, across TV, radio, and podcasts, is a masterclass in pausing, reviewing, and refining. She's spoken about the nerves that come with every new season, and the discomfort of hearing yourself back. But also about the value of showing up again anyway, changed by what you've learned. "I started out Season One thinking I knew say things like, "If you have a story to share, I want to hear it," or "Let me know what you think," and you get the sense she genuinely means it.

She doesn't stop there. Jennifer's social feeds and blog are full of shoutouts to listeners and guests who've followed up, shared resources, or sparked new ideas (*Cult of Pedagogy*, 2024). She'll often highlight a great question or comment from a listener, turning it into a springboard for the next conversation. Her DMs are open, her inbox is busy, and her podcast is a living, breathing community project.

Jennifer teaches us that it's not about asking questions for the sake of it, it's asking to genuinely connect, learn, and keep the story rolling. Jennifer Gonzalez has turned asking into art.

The Best Hosts Keep Asking

The job of asking doesn't end when the mic turns off. Some of the most important questions come *after* the conversation.

When you ask with purpose afterwards, you:

- Give stories a second life. Get permission to share, building trust and letting powerful moments travel further.
- Turn one conversation into many. Open doors you didn't even know were there by asking for a simple referral or share request.
- Keep the dialogue alive. Turn a one-off interaction into something meaningful, memorable, and ongoing.

Keep on asking.

It's not about asking questions for the sake of it, it's asking to genuinely connect, learn, and keep the story rolling.

Try this:

- After an event, workshop, or episode, send a quick message. Try, "I'd love to hear what stuck with you most?" or, "Was there a moment that really landed for you?" Keep it short, curious, and open.
- Use their response to keep the conversation alive. Next time you connect, refer back to it, "You mentioned X last time, we could build on that." It shows you listened and makes them feel seen.
- Track the patterns. If the same phrase, story, or section keeps coming up, pay attention. That's your resonance. That's your repeatable gold. And it's also where you might want to double down.

The moment someone names what landed for them, they remember it better. And so do you!

Learning from Legends: Jennifer Gonzalez – The Ripple Effect

Let's talk about the art of asking. And not just any asking, asking that could turn a moment into a movement. If you want to see this in action, look no further than Jennifer Gonzalez, host of *Cult of Pedagogy* (Gonzalez, 2024). It may look like she's running a podcast, but really, she's running a global staffroom.

I'll admit, I came late to the party, but after two episodes, I could understand attraction. Jennifer is a champion at drawing people in and keeping the conversation going, long after the episode ends.

She's not afraid to ask for more. At the end of her show, she'll invite you to reach out, share your thoughts, send her a message, or even suggest a future guest (Gonzalez, 2024). You'll hear her

travelled (Johnson and Smith, 2023). Apparently, subtle hints are overrated. Just ask.

Try this:
- Ask your guest, "What part of this conversation do you think your network would love to hear?"
- Ask your audience, "Who else should I be talking to?"
- Make sharing easy; provide a snippet, a key quote, or direct link they can copy, cut, and post.

Create Memories

Want to know what people remember? Ask them. Want to know how they felt? Ask that too.

It might feel a bit obvious, but the results aren't. A 2023 study led by cognitive psychologist Dr Melinda Brown and her team at the University of Queensland found that when people are prompted to reflect on a specific moment after an event, whether it's a story, idea, or emotion, it doesn't just help them remember it, it makes them like it more. Ooo, that's good. Their brains literally tag the memory as more meaningful. The researchers tracked how follow-up reflection influenced people's recall and emotional response over time. The result showed higher satisfaction, stronger memory, and increased likelihood of re-engaging later (Brown et al., 2023).

In short, if you ask someone, "What stuck with you?", they're more likely to remember it, feel good about it, and come back for more. It goes far beyond simply extending the conversation; it makes it better.

Plus, by prompting reflection, you're also giving yourself insight into what actually resonated. That is going to be very very useful.

further (Smith et al., 2024). Which makes it sound like consent is contagious! I really hope science is right on this one.

Try this:

- Send a quick check-in message before you share a standout moment. Ask, "I loved this part of our chat, are you happy for me to share it in a post?" It takes ten seconds and builds trust that lasts much longer
- If you're running an event, get permission upfront. Do it verbally *and* in writing (a simple release form will do). Try, "Some of the best ideas today will come from you. If you share something great, are you okay with us sharing it more widely?"
- If someone hesitates, respect the hesitation. Don't push. Don't reframe. Just move on. Trust is always more valuable than content. Always.

Promotion and Referrals

People won't automatically share an episode, event, or interview – even when they love it. They won't always send another great guest your way, even if they've got the ideal candidate. But they will if we ask.

In good news for those of us who hate being pushy: science says asking works. In 2023, network scientists Dr Claire Johnson and Professor Alan Smith (who study the actual dynamics of how ideas and influence spread) ran a series of experiments on what makes people share. They found that direct requests like "Can you share this?" or "Know anyone else I should speak to?" dramatically increased both the number of responses and how far the message after. But those ripples only start if you throw out a few stones! That is, ask your audience to do some things. In this instance, they did. Not because they were polite, but because the questions activated something.

Psychologists call this the *generation effect*, a term coined by Slamecka and Graf (1978), who found that people remember content far better when they *generate* it themselves instead of just consuming it. Basically, when people get involved, their brain says, "Ooh, this matters!"

It's not just about memory, either. There's another concept called *self-generated validity* (Feldman and Lynch, 1988), which shows that people believe what they say out loud more than what they hear. When you ask them to reflect, they're more likely to follow through on it later.

So, while the mic may be off, your influence is not. Here's how to ask like it matters, because it does.

Permission to Share

Just because someone shares a story in the moment doesn't mean they want it broadcast beyond the room.

Asking, "Can I share this?" does two things. First, it gives them ownership over their voice and more often than not, they'll say yes. Secondly, they'll keep an eye out for it and be ready to re-share it themselves.

This isn't just good manners (although it's that too), it's science. In a 2024 study, communications researcher Dr Samantha Smith and her team set out to measure the impact of consent on audience trust. Turns out, when people know a story was shared *with permission*, they're significantly more likely to trust it and share it

The Art of Asking – How the Right Questions Turn Moments into Movements

A few years ago, I was sitting in Canberra airport, sipping a glass of sparkling wine (meant to be coffee, but the moment called for bubbles). I'd just hosted a keynote.

I know you're meant to give keynotes, but it feels more like hosting to me. Even when I'm telling a story on stage, I can't help but start pulling people into the conversation. Blame years of talk-back radio.

That day, the room was buzzing. People seemed engaged, and I walked off stage feeling like I'd done my job. But it was what happened next that stayed with me.

As I sat in the quiet of the airport lounge, my inbox started pinging. One attendee was thanking me and introducing me to someone they thought I should meet. Another was sharing what had stuck with them. Over on social media, I was being tagged in posts of people wearing outfits that made them feel confident (which was something I'd mentioned during the talk).

That's when it hit me. The conversation with this audience wasn't over. While the keynote had been engaging, it wasn't what made people act. It was the questions I'd asked at the end.

Before walking off stage, I'd done something I hadn't always been so intentional about. I asked the audience to connect with me. I invited them to share what resonated. I explicitly asked them to tag me on social media (which still makes me cringe), and they actually did! I asked them to introduce me to someone they thought I should know, and they did that too!

And sitting there in the airport, I realised: the value of a conversation isn't just in what happens during it. It's in the ripples that come really is, I think, is a public, yet also private and playful way of saying thank you for being part of our show.

When it comes to highlights, they're the kings. Their "Remembering Project/s" and best-of shows are a celebration of the best moments that they want you to remember; literally, it's in the title. (*Remembering Project*, 2024). Plus, the best bits are spotlighted on socials, showing the faces behind the mics, the stunts and the stories.

The real magic of *The Share* isn't just in the thank you or the feedback, it's in making people feel like they're part of something bigger. Hamish and Andy didn't follow anyone else's script. They created their own rituals, their own language, their own way of making every listener, guest, and random passerby feel like they're in on the joke and in the club. That's what turns a show into a community.

So, when you're thinking about how to share after the show, celebrate the best bits, replay the wild moments, be generous with your gratitude and feedback and let everyone know you're in this together.

The Best Hosts Make Moments Matter

Great hosts share the love.

- Gratitude strengthens relationships.
- Feedback shapes how people feel about the experience.
- Highlights define the lasting impact.

When you take the time to shape how a conversation is remembered, you create something people want to come back to.

Let's move from sharing to asking and unpack the key questions to ask after you host.

When you choose what to spotlight, you help shape the legacy of the conversation and how others remember it. You can make specific moments matter on purpose.

- Weave the takeaways into your follow-up. Mention them in thank-you emails, episode intros, or next-meeting agendas. It shows you were paying attention and helps others do the same.
- Refer back to them next time you host, as is appropriate. Bring the thread full circle. When you echo something later, it tells the audience: *This mattered. Pay attention.*

When you choose what to spotlight, you help shape the legacy of the conversation and how others remember it. You can make specific moments matter on purpose.

Learning from Legends: Hamish and Andy – Let Everyone in on the Joke

Listening to the Hamish and Andy Podcast on Thursdays is the little bit of light in my week that I didn't know I needed. I love it. For years, I didn't listen, then I re-found them, and honestly, what a delight they are to listen to amongst a sea of hot takes and hustle. It took maybe two episodes, and I was in. While the show is full of in-jokes, the way they share them makes you feel like you're part of the gang almost instantly. That means they don't just have listeners; they have a community, and it's all in how they share the fun (*Hamish & Andy*, 2024).

Hamish and Andy have built their own version of "the share." While I don't expect they're sending out many formal thank you notes, what they do is hand out are bows. Seriously. If you go up to them in the street and ask for a dollar, if they don't have one, they will give you a bow. Not the thing you tie in your shoelaces, the thing you do at the end of a concert. They will physically lean down and bow for you. While it's got the bones of a great gag, what it

It's about more than being nice. It's about building confidence, trust, and stronger guests, one honest compliment at a time.

Shape the Narrative

What people remember most about a conversation often isn't the hour they sat in the room, it's the story they continue to tell afterwards. As hosts, we get to shape that story. The details they carry forward, the moments they retell, the lines that stick, aren't accidental. They're usually the part we've chosen to spotlight. The narrative we've shaped on purpose.

This is where the *Recency Effect* comes in. Cognitive scientist Bennet Murdock (1962) found that when people are given a list of items, they're more likely to remember the last few. The same goes for conversations: we remember what we heard last and what stood out most.

That final word is ours to shape, and it's often the one that lasts. This isn't simply the conclusion or wrap-up that happens when we're on stage, in the meeting or behind the mic. It's how we talk about the key moments afterwards.

Try this:

Before you pack up or prep the next event:

- Write down three sharp takeaways from the conversation. Not just what was said but what *landed*. What felt fresh? What made people laugh, nod, go quiet? That's the gold.
- Turn one of those into something shareable. A post. A pull quote. An email opener. A teaser for the next episode. It doesn't need to go viral; it just needs to capture the tone and truth of the moment.

Give Feedback

Same goes for feedback. If gratitude is about *recognition*, feedback is about *growth*. Oprah once said that no matter who her guest was — presidents, celebrities, everyday people — they all asked the same thing after the cameras stopped rolling: "How did I do?" (*The Independent*, 2017). Whether we admit it or not, we *all* want to know if we made an impact.

As the host, we're in a prime position to give it. Not to critique, but to *lift*. To help someone feel seen, valued, and even better equipped for the next conversation.

Organisational psychologist Marshall Goldsmith (2003) coined the term *feedforward*; the idea that future-focused feedback works better than picking apart what's already happened. It's less threatening. More useful. And, frankly, more fun to give.

So, skip the vague praise or awkward silence. Your guest just did something brave. Help them see what worked and what could grow.

Try this:

After each interview or event, tell your guest one thing that really landed and one thing they might build on.

- "You gave such clear examples; I could see the audience nodding along. Collect more of these to share in your next interview."
- "Your pacing was great once you hit your stride. Next time, let's find a stronger open so you get there faster."
- "That moment when you paused before answering? Powerful. More of that, please."

Plus, for the person receiving it, a thoughtful thank you triggers the same feel-good chemicals as getting a reward. Like a hug for your nervous system.

Importantly, generic gratitude doesn't stick. The key is specificity. The more personal and precise your thanks, the more memorable and meaningful it becomes.

Try this:

Before moving on to the next task, take 60 seconds to show someone they mattered. It's more than thanks. It's telling someone, "I saw what you did, and here's why it made a difference."

- "Thanks for joining me" is fine. "It was so valuable having you here. The way you told that story about your first job completely reframed the topic for me. I'm really grateful for that." is better.
- "Great episode" is nice. "Thank you for lifting the energy. Your laughter in that second segment, that's the moment people will replay. It changed the energy in the best way" is gold.
- "Nice work today" is polite. "Thank you for the calm you brought today. The way you grounded the room before that hard question? I learned from that, and I'm going to try it" is unforgettable.

While people may not remember the specifics of your words, it's often your words that create a specific feeling. That is what they remember. That is what brings them back. That is what creates your reputation as a great host. Give gratitude generously.

interview of our life, and still leave people cold if the ending feels rushed, flat, or forgotten. But nail the final few beats? That's what lingers. That's what shapes the memory.

We've seen this play out in big ways:

- Trevor Noah didn't just leave *The Daily Show*; he used his final monologue to reflect on what the experience had meant to him and his audience (2022, December 8).
- Leigh Sales didn't just step away from *7:30*; she delivered a heartfelt farewell that highlighted the best content, the team, the guests, and the audience, reinforcing the show's legacy (2022, June 30).
- Oprah didn't just end her talk show; she turned the entire final season into a celebration of its impact (2010 – 2011).

We expect this from well-known hosts, but I reckon a version of this type of sharing happens after every event, show, or meeting. Here's how to do that effectively.

Give Gratitude

Public thanks are great, but real gratitude is often best delivered privately. In fact, gratitude is one of the sneakiest superpowers a host can have, because it works both ways.

Psychologists Robert Emmons and Michael McCullough (2003) found that when people made gratitude a regular habit, not just a once-a-year card or a quick "Cheers", they felt happier, slept better, and even exercised more. Who knew that thanking someone might actually make you do more squats?

The Share – Shaping How Your Hosting Is Remembered

Let's be honest. Despite what I've said above, most of us still treat hosting like a performance. You prep, you deliver, you pack down, and you're onto the next gig before the applause has even faded.

But, to retrofit one of the most beautiful and well-known quotes Maya Angelou has delivered, the audience might forget what you said, the guest might forget what they did, but no one will forget how it made them feel.

Those feelings are, more often than not, shaped in the aftermath. Yep. After, not during. The moment when the lights are down, the room is half-empty, and you're deciding whether to bolt or to build.

Psychologists Daniel Kahneman, Barbara Fredrickson, and colleagues weren't exactly studying podcasts when they coined the Peak-End Rule (1993), but they may as well have been. They discovered that when people reflect on an experience, they don't average it out. They judge it based on two key moments:

- The most emotionally intense point (the *peak*).
- The way it finished (the *end*).

In their experiments, even people who endured discomfort (like sticking their hands in freezing water) *preferred* a longer experience if it ended just a bit better. That's right. A slightly less awful ending made the whole thing feel more positive.

What does that mean for us?

It means we could host a perfect event, deliver the smoothest about the mic being on. It's about what happens when it's off. The way you carry the conversation forward. The space you create for others to join in after. The way you let it shape *you*, not just the audience.

That's what this final part is about. Because, while there's a tendency to want to pack up and move on, there is a specific skill in finding the momentum. The extra juice. Identifying the real impact and value of the moment you just hosted, that, if handled well, will make change happen.

Here's what that looks like:

- You **share wisely**: offering real thanks, giving real feedback, and shaping what people remember.
- You **ask with purpose**: securing permission, planting future seeds, and keeping conversations alive long after the formal end
- You **reflect with intent**: getting curious, adjusting what needs tweaking, and embedding those lessons that make you stronger every time.

I like to think of hosting as less of a performance and more of a practice. Yep, like yoga. We're continually practising. And the after part is where the practice compounds. For fellow yogis, it's Savasana.

After

What Happens After Is What Makes You Better

I once did a live broadcast from the women's prison in Tasmania. It's still one of the most extraordinary days I've ever had behind the mic. It wasn't a stunt. It wasn't about ratings. It was a chance to open the gates, literally and metaphorically, and let the audience into a place most would never otherwise get to see.

There was so much to consider. The stories. The system. The purpose. The potential impact on victims who might be listening. We walked in aware of the weight of it all. But what I didn't expect, what I couldn't have predicted, was how much of the *real* impact came after.

I've never had so many phone calls, texts, emails, and real-life conversations about a broadcast. People reached out for days, sometimes weeks, afterwards. Sharing what they'd heard. Asking questions. Offering their own stories. The ripple was bigger than anything I'd felt before.

This experience showed me something I've never forgotten: the power of a conversation isn't just in how it happens, it's also in how it's shared, afterwards.

That prison broadcast reminded me that hosting is never just

Where the Mic Comes Alive

You're ready. You've done the setup. You've calibrated, curated, and prepared. But prep can only take you so far.

Once the mic is on, the job of hosting shifts. It's no longer about what you've planned, it's about what you *create*. It's about how you hold the moment. How you move with it. How you bring people with you without stealing the spotlight.

And now, you've got the tools to do exactly that.

- **Rituals**: you've built habits that keep you on time, grounded, and ready for anything.
- **Rapport**: you know how to work in harmony, so your guest feels seen and safe.
- **Route**: you have The Question Compass to help you find your path, pivot when needed, and go deeper without getting lost.

These are the skills that stop a conversation from falling flat. They help you avoid being the kind of host who clings too tightly or lets things drift.

You're no longer burnt, dry, raw, or slick. You're great. Great Toast. A Great Toast Host. Structured but flexible. Engaging but natural. Present but not pushy.

You're the kind of host people feel safe with and remember. But your job's not done yet. Because what happens *after* the conversation ends? When the room empties, the mics turn off, and the slides go blank? That's when the best hosts do something most don't. That's when they create momentum.

interrogate; she invites. She does this so well that her guests end up sharing stories they probably didn't even know they had! It's a joy to listen to.

That's no accident. Sarah usually starts light, lets her guests settle, and listens like her life depends on it. She doesn't bulldoze her way to the "heavy stuff." She waits, pays attention to the space between the words, and when the time is right, nudges the conversation through a gate nobody else even spotted.

As author Charlotte Wood said after her interview with Sarah: "That was one of the most attentive, intelligent, and emotionally astute interviews I've ever had" (Wood, 2019). Which is exactly the vibe we're going for, isn't it?

Sarah uses the Compass instinctively. She searches, extracts, clarifies, and expands – never in a straight line and never with pressure. But this isn't just a tool for discovery interviews like Sarah's. It works for accountability interviews too. Sometimes you need a gentle nudge, sometimes it takes firm push to get them through that gate. The art is knowing which one the moment calls for. Once you get to know the Compass, you'll understand how many applications it has in everyday work and life. From interview prep to meeting agendas, live facilitation to real conversations, performance reviews to stakeholder surveys and the rest. Eventually, you'll develop your internal compass (which I've kindly made external for now), allowing you to help your guests and audiences walk through the right gates, willingly.

So, next time you're hosting, channel your inner Kanowski. Use your Question Compass. Open the right gate, at the right time, and watch the conversation wander somewhere wonderful.

you really refine your skills, you hear the third voice. The voice of your audience.

The third voice is like an invisible director in your ear. It asks:

- What does the audience want to know next?
- What does the audience think is missing from this answer?
- Where does the audience need this conversation to go next?

Keep an ear out for the third voice. When you hear it, you'll know you're well on your way.

Mastering the Route

If you want better answers, start with better questions. Better questions come from knowing which gate to open, when, and for whom. So go on. Become a Chief Gate Opener. Take your audience somewhere they've never been before.

Learning from Legends: Sarah Kanowski – Find the Gate, Open It Gently

I spent more than a few hours listening to the craft of interviewing while I was developing the Question Compass, and the ABC's Sarah Kanowski was firmly in the rotation. While Sarah hasn't seen my Compass (yet!), if you listen to her on ABC's *Conversations*, you'd swear she's got a copy tucked under her headphones.

Sarah's interviews are a masterclass in opening gates, sometimes wide, sometimes narrow, sometimes so gently you barely notice you've stepped into a whole new paddock. She doesn't

If you want better answers,
start with better questions.

That's why I teach this live, in person, in the mess of real dialogue. It's game-changing and gate-opening.

That said, you can have a play right now.

Try this:

- Listen back to a great interview and place each question into a quadrant. Was the host searching, extracting, clarifying, or expanding? Where they looking for experiences, details, beliefs or ideas?
- Prepare for your next interview and write three primary questions for each quadrant. Where might you start, and where might you take the conversation?
- Experiment with balance. If you always start in one quadrant, mix it up. See what happens when you shift directions earlier or later than usual.

I'm sure I'll get into primary and secondary questions in another book. For now, focus on mastering the *route*. Because once you do, you'll always know which gate to open.

"The key to a great interview is preparation, curiosity, and the ability to listen and respond in the moment."

– Leigh Sales, former host of 7.30

Bonus: Listening for the Third Voice

There was a point in my career when I started hearing *the third voice*. At first, hosting is about listening to your guests. Then, you start hearing yourself, crafting responses in real time. But once

Example:

Reflections: "What's been your biggest learning from the whole experience?"

Possibilities: "How could that shape what happens next time?"

The diagonals are all about instinct. They follow the natural intuition of a great interviewer: the pull to search, the urge to extract the gold, the need to clarify, or the want to create and expand. It's less about ticking boxes or following a formula, and more about echolocating and feeling where the conversation wants to go next.

Using the Compass in Real Time

How we use the Question Compass depends on a few things: the type of conversation we're hosting, who's listening, and who's sitting across from us.

While a balanced mix of all four quadrants is the dream, we need to expect that every conversation will have its own shape. Some need a lighter, future-focused vibe. Others ask you to go deep and sit with the heavier stuff. Whereas others need clarity and accountability.

We might spend the whole conversation dancing between just two quadrants. That's not a problem. But if the energy dips, or the answers start feeling same-same, the compass helps us switch it up without losing the thread.

Importantly, this is a planning tool, a real-time guide, and a mirror! The Question Compass can reveal the patterns in *our* questioning style. Do you always stay light? Dive too deep, too fast? Avoid detail? Forget to go wide (or wild)? It helps us notice habits. Once we notice, we can steer with more intention.

But you won't master this from a diagram in a book. You learn it by doing. In real conversations. With real humans. In the moment.

North-West | Extracting Mode | Stories and Specifics

After searching, we jump into extracting mode and pull out the gold. The vivid, concrete stories and specifics that make an interview compelling. While we're searching, we'll hear... something; a moment that hasn't quite been unpacked, an urge to want to know more, a 'hang on a minute, what?' That's when we go in. These questions help us draw out concrete moments. Snapshots. Things the audience can picture, remember and repeat. It's where the story becomes tangible and where a moment turns into a memory.

Example:

Stories: "What do you remember about them moment when...?"
Specifics: "Specifically, who was involved?"

South-West | Clarifying Mode | Opinions and Perspectives

This mode is all about getting clarity, leaving no space for assumptions. We're helping the guest explain what they really think. We're clarifying their take. Both their surface-level opinion and their deeper perspective. It's great for surfacing tensions, clarifying their thinking, and revealing where people stand. These questions bring clarity to beliefs and decisions.

Example:

Opinions: "So, what's your take?"
Perspectives: "What's this really all about?"

South-East | Expanding Mode | Reflections and Possibilities

After we've narrowed in to get the clarity, we then open things up again. We're helping the guest expand their thinking to reflect on what they've learned and to imagine what could be next. It's where hindsight meets vision. It allows people to explore their values and ideas without the limitations of reality.

us anchor to that intention. They're practical. Focused. Outcome-aware. The stuff of orienteers.

But conversations aren't always linear. And we don't always know where we want them to go or what we need to find out. Sometimes, we just need to tune into the moment, trust our instincts and feel our way forward. That's where the diagonals come in. This is bat territory.

Navigating the Diagonals

The best hosts know how to ride that rhythm of a conversation without making it feel like they're looking for something in particular, but rather learning along with everyone else. This is why I find the diagonals, liberating! They allow us to embrace the idea that we don't know what we don't know.

If the standard couplings help us focus on the outcomes we need, the diagonals let us focus on the mode we're in as the question asker. Let's break them down.

North-East | Searching Mode | Circumstance and Influences

This is a great place to start. As a host, this is when we're in searching mode, finding out what's going on in our guests' world *and* the wider one. This is about gathering context, both the big ideas that have influenced our guest and their personal circumstances that have shaped them. It blends external and internal influences. Importantly, when we're in this mode and asking these questions, we're searching for something valuable to extract.

Example:

Influences: "What was *the* situation?

Circumstances: What was *your* situation?"

conviction, and tension lives. We gravitate here when we're trying to understand someone's frame or what's driving their choices. These are the questions that uncover the meaning our guest made of the moments we've just unpacked. These questions draw out beliefs, insights, and personal truths. They're about interpretation, not information. We're not asking what happened, we're asking what's shifted because of it.

Example:

Perspectives: "What do you think it was really about?"

Reflections: "Looking back now, what did you learn?"

Ideas (Influences and Possibilities)

This part of the compass takes the focus away from the personal experience and beliefs and into the external world. These questions invite discussions of big ideas and world views, while also diving into imagination and new ways of seeing. We use them when people are stuck in the now or the known, and we want to loosen their thinking or help them see something new. These are great for drawing out big-picture thinking, examining systems, or breaking out of stuck patterns.

Example:

Influence: "What else may have had an influence?"

Possibility: "If you had a magic wand, what would you change? What else? And then what?"

The standard couplings are really useful when we know what types of answers we need. We can use them to prepare for a conversation, knowing this tool will help us draw out everything we need and more. Are we looking for an experience? A belief? An idea? The detail? All of the above? The standard couplings help

Experiences (Stories and Circumstances)

Are you trying to bring the moment to life? Do you want to know what happened and what it felt like to be there? Then head north. What you're looking for is experiences. These questions dive into scenes from someone's life. They help you to start in action with a story or set the scene with the background circumstances. They're great at removing any assumptions we or the audience may have and are usually the most memorable parts of any interview or conversation.

Example:

Circumstances: "What was happening in your life at the time?"

Stories: "What's a moment from that time that you still think about?"

Details (Specifics and Solutions)

This pairing is about *zooming in*. Either on a particular moment in a story to make it clearer, sharper, more tangible, or on an opinion or next step, to get moving. We might jump to these questions if someone has skimmed over details, we feel like we're missing something, or we want them to say a particular thing out loud.

There is no room for waffle here. These questions help avoid assumptions, get the facts straight, or translate big thinking into tangible action.

Example:

Specifics: "If we go back to that moment, who else was there?"
Opinions: "What do you think caused the problem?"

Beliefs (Perspectives and Reflections)

Ok, now you want to know what is really behind their thinking, not just what happened. This is values territory. It's where pathology,

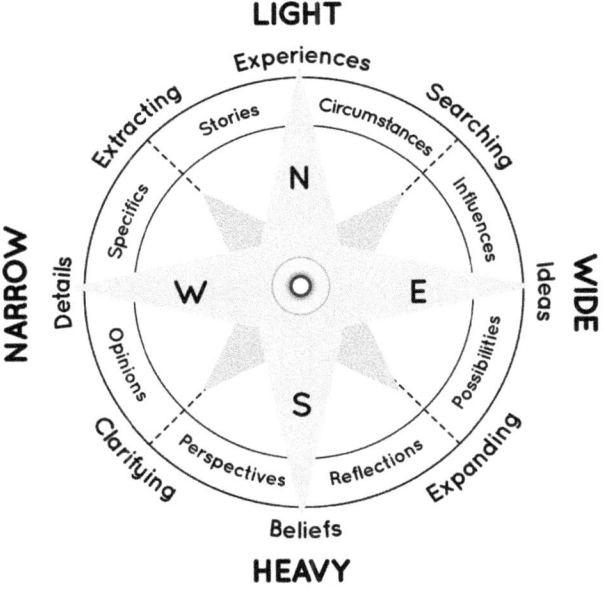

The Standard Couplings

Most hosts don't sit around thinking, "Hmm... I need a light question right now." I've never caught myself saying, "Time to go heavy and really lean in." That's not how real conversations work. A great place to begin is with what I've dubbed the *standard couplings*. This approach is more deliberate, more outcome-oriented. Are we after a real experience? A big idea? A personal belief? The details? The question becomes the catalyst that will surface the thing we're really looking for.

The standard couplings are questions that draw out the responses you'll find at true North, East, South, and West. Each question type on the Compass is paired with its counterpart. These pairs are helpful when you're planning, guiding, or even rescuing a conversation. They give you a quick shorthand for what you're trying to uncover and what kind of question might help you get there.

Wide questions draw out:

- Influences: external forces and broader context.
- Possibilities: what-ifs, visions, and new thinking.
- Reflections: insights, personal learning, shifts in perspective.
- Circumstances: layered context, personal and environmental clues.

West – Narrow Questions

West tightens the focus. These questions bring structure, clarity, and decision points. This is where we can direct our guests down a certain path, and where we eliminate assumptions. They're precise and great for getting concrete details, but they can feel a bit blunt if asked too early.

Use them to dig out gold, focus the guest, or move things forward. These types of questions draw out:

- Stories: concrete descriptions of events, memories and moments.
- Specifics: detailed facts and clear definitions.
- Opinions: suggested actions and personal reactions.
- Perspectives: beliefs that have been translated into reasoning

As you can see, some questions are light and narrow, others heavy and wide. All of them are useful and play a role in getting the best from a conversation.

- Stories: vivid moments, events, and memories.
- Circumstances: settings, contexts, and important background.
- Specifics: factual details or precise moments.
- Influences: external factors that have influenced the moment.

South – Heavy Questions

The southern half of the compass takes us deeper. If the north is about information, the south is about interpretation. These are the meaning-makers. This is how we find out what our guests made those real moments mean. This is where we ask someone to interpret, reflect, or take a stand.

They often carry emotional weight, not in a dramatic way, but in the way they invite personal truth. We don't usually start here. We often need to earn our way here. Heavy questions draw out:

- Opinions: preferences, judgements, the quote.
- Perspectives: beliefs, pathology, and points of view.
- Reflections: insights, takeaways, and internal shifts.
- Possibilities: imagined futures, dreams and ideal scenarios.

East – Wide Questions

This side of the compass gives the guest plenty of space to choose where to take the conversation next. These questions create surprising threads, bonus tangents, and invite exploration of options, patterns, connections, and big ideas. They're expansive. Curious. Non-linear. The opposite of leading. Great when you need blue-sky thinking or a fresh angle and don't want to make any assumptions.

Researchers talk about something called the *funnel technique*; starting broad before narrowing. It's a favourite in user experience and design thinking – start wide to gather lots of insight, then slowly home in on what matters most. Sounds very neat in theory. But real conversations? Not so much.

Real conversations don't naturally funnel down like an ice cream cone. I've never found a funnel of questions that's flexible enough to work with real conversations. Which is why I think we're better off with a compass. Something that helps us shift direction in real time without losing our way.

Let's get our bearings.

The Four Key Directions

Think of the Question Compass as a mental map. It shows us all the directions the conversation may go and gives us a way to choose on the fly without losing the plot. It tells us what type of question will get us what we need, depending on where we are... and where we want to go. Let's start by unpacking the four key directions, each one nudging the conversation into a different kind of territory.

North – Light Questions

The entire top half of the compass is quite light. These are the questions that feel easy (or obvious) to ask and are often easy (or obvious) to answer. But don't confuse 'light' and 'easy' with 'fluffy'. The reason they feel light is because they are about real things, actual events that people can explain or describe.

They help guests feel seen, safe, and grounded before we go deeper. These questions draw out:

Questions are a lot like gates. Some questions are light and easy to ask. Others can feel heavy to ask and remain heavy until an outcome or learning is found. Some open our brains to big pastures, while others lead us along a particular road.

open paddocks full of grass. Others funnel them into narrow lane-ways. And their behaviour will adjust accordingly.

I reckon my expertise in gate opening informed my expertise in question asking. Questions are a lot like gates. Some questions are light and easy to ask. Others can feel heavy to ask and remain heavy until an outcome or learning is found. Some open our brains to big pastures, while others lead us along a particular road.

Just like a great C.G.O. knows which gate to open at which moment, a great host knows which question to ask at which stage of the conversation. The Question Compass is the tool that helps you get your bearings. It helps you find the right question, at the right time, for the right purpose.

The Question Compass

The Question Compass can be really useful during preparation, helping you plan your route and consider the directions your conversation may go. However, the real value of the Question Compass kicks in *during* the conversation. Because even with the best intentions, it's easy to get lost. You follow an unexpected thread. The guest surprises you. You blank on what comes next. Suddenly, you're knee-deep in waffle with no exit strategy.

Every great conversation moves in multiple directions. However, I've found it's not as it feels. The questions that lead conversations tend to follow patterns. It's worth noting that we all have our own default question-asking patterns, and they're not always useful. Some of us prefer to start wide and light, while others start narrow and deep. Facilitators love the wide side, while interrogators stay narrow. Content creators stay light, while ther-apists get heavy.

questions their whole life, right? Right. Whether or not they're good at it hardly gets a thought.

This is why I developed The Question Compass™: a tool to help hosts (or anyone) navigate conversations using great questions. It helps us to follow a specific route or direction, or adventure into unknown territory, and always be confident that we can take a detour and find our way back.

In this section, I'll run you through the basics so you can get your bearings. But full disclosure: this bit is steeped in practice. As in, you need to actually do it. Repeatedly. On real people. Or maybe you could start with... gates, like I did. Shall I explain?

Creating the Compass

You might assume The Question Compass was born from my years as a radio presenter, podcaster, and panel facilitator. Or maybe you'd guess it came from my work as an event MC, executive mentor, or coach. Fair guess, but no.

Its roots go much further back... to my very first job. When I was a kid, I used to 'go to work' with Dad on the farm, and my job was Chief Gate Opener (aka: C.G.O.). Don't laugh — a C.G.O. deals with important and often tricky business. As Chief Gate Opener, there were lots of different sorts of gates I'd have to know how to open. Because on a farm, not all gates are the same.

Some are perfectly balanced, easy to unhook and swing open. On others, the hinges are rusted, or the strainer post isn't straight, and you have to lift the full weight of the gate just to budge it, and keep holding the weight until all the animals are through. Plus, when opening gates for stock, you have to consider where they're coming from and where they're going to. Some gates lead into big

That's the thing about rapport. It's not always about making people comfortable. It's about making them feel safe enough to be uncomfortable.

That's the thing about rapport. It's not always about making people comfortable. It's about making them feel safe enough to be uncomfortable.

If you want to score high on the Rapport Card, commit to:

- Connecting quickly so trust is built fast.
- Reflecting naturally so the energy feels in sync.
- Directing subtly so the conversation flows effortlessly.

The best conversations, like the best harmonies, blend voices while letting each one shine. So next time you host, channel your inner Finn Brother. Find the harmony and enjoy the magic you create with your guest. Your audience will love it.

The Route – Questions that Take You Somewhere Real

You've made it. You've reached the part where we focus on the interview itself. This is where we get stuck into the craft of asking questions so it sounds natural yet mindblowing. It's the ultimate paradox; making something sound off-the-cuff takes a ridiculous amount of effort, and, cuff.

Most of us have had some basic training in question-asking. We tend to be given the classic open vs. closed question breakdown. When I was first taught this, I distinctly remember thinking, "But that can't be it, can it?" If you've thought the same, you were right to wonder. There's so much more nuance to asking great questions. Explaining or teaching that nuance can be tricky, plus many people think they've already got the skill. I mean, they've been asking

It's less about creating the conversation and more about creating space for the conversation.

Learning from Legends: Marc Fennell – The Art of Tuning In

If there's anyone who knows how to move between quick wit and quiet resonance without breaking stride, it's Marc Fennell.

He's hosted everything from *The Feed* and *Mastermind Australia* to the award-winning podcast *Stuff the British Stole*, and no matter the format, his conversations are always grounded, human, and real. But that smooth delivery is no accident. It's the result of active, deliberate rapport-building.

In multiple interviews, including his own episodes of *Stop Everything!* on ABC Radio National, Marc has reflected on the importance of meeting people where they are. He's spoken about the moments when you can feel a guest tense up or go into 'performance mode', and how he gently pulls them back into a space where they can just be themselves.

One of his signature techniques is to go further than just asking a question. He makes sure he phrases it in a way that shows the guest he's done the work. That he understands them. That he's *with* them.

Take his *Stuff the British Stole* interview with Māori broadcaster Mihingarangi Forbes. The topic was complex and heavy: cultural trauma, colonial legacy, and sacred artefacts. But Marc wasn't rigid. He listened. Reflected. Let silence hang when it needed to. He shifted tone without shifting the trust. It felt like a real exchange, not a performance.

In a 2021 interview with *The Sydney Morning Herald*, Marc explained it this way: "I don't want my guests to feel like they're on trial. I want them to feel like they're in good hands. That I've created a space for something honest to happen."

feel guided instead of grilled, they're far more likely to share the good stuff: their real thoughts, personal stories, and honest insights. The secret sauce is a mix of strategic silence and soft redirection (Friedman and Riggio, 1982). It's hosting that whispers, "You're safe here. Say the thing."

Try this:

- Play with pauses. Use the five-second rule. When your guest finishes speaking, count (silently) to five before you jump in. It'll feel long. It's not. Often, they'll fill that space themselves, and *that's* where the gold is. Let the silence do the work.

- Use generous prompts. Instead of, "Can you answer the question?", try, "That's a great insight, can you take us a little deeper on...", or "You mentioned X, what happened next?" These keep the energy open without course-correcting too hard.

- Spot the story hiding inside the waffle. If your guest is circling a point or veering off-track, you don't have to shut it down. Instead, try: "That's such an interesting angle, how does that connect to...", or "You said something a moment ago I don't want to miss..." You're redirecting with care, not control.

- Stack questions carefully. One question. One idea. Then wait. Don't overexplain or give them a menu of options. Keep it clear so they don't feel the need to guess what you want.

- Read your ratio. After the session, listen back. Whose voice did you hear more, yours or theirs? Aim to make your words support, not dominate.

People don't open up when they feel pushed, they open up when they feel safe.

- Adjust on the fly. If their pace shifts, shift with them. If they get excited, join the fun. If they lean in, lounge back, or look around, mirror their body with yours – subtly, again, without being weird.
- Practise in everyday conversations. Match the pace of a slow speaker, then an energetic one. Copy your partner, kids, or friends over dinner. See if they notice. It'll be fun.

Rapport not only sounds great, it feels great too and makes for a much better experience for everyone.

Direct Without Pushing

The best hosts aren't interrogators. But they also aren't passengers. Our job is to steer the conversation without making it feel like we're steering. It's as if we are driving a dodgem car, but rather than trying to compete with the others, we're driving alongside them, giving subtle nudges to keep things moving without anyone feeling jolted.

That means:

- Giving space: let guests talk without jumping in too soon.
- Using silence strategically: some of the best moments come after a pause.
- Gently guiding: if a guest wanders off-topic, bring them back without shutting them down.

This is where the real magic happens. People don't open up when they feel pushed, they open up when they feel safe.

Social psychologist Howard Friedman spent years exploring what he called 'conversational leadership'. The kind that makes people want to open up, not clam up. He found that when people

When you build connection through tiny, intentional signals in the first few moments, the rest (of the moments) will thank you.

Reflect Like a Mirror

Let's unpack what's going on when you meet someone who just gets you. When they kind of feel *like* you. They're not mimicking, they're matching. It's called, mirroring. Mmmmm.

It's the art of subtly matching someone's tone, body language, or pace so they feel comfortable, understood, and open. When done right, it makes a conversation feel effortless, like you've both tuned into the same frequency.

Another official term for this is The Chameleon Effect. Cute, right? Coined by psychologist Tanya Chartrand and neuroscientist John Bargh, this charming bit of science shows how even a tiny head tilt or a subtle vocal match can boost likeability and build trust (Chartrand and Bargh, 1999). It's biological magic!

Our brain has a built-in copycat switch called the mirror neuron system. It fires up when we watch someone else move, react, or emote. This means we do some of this stuff subconsciously, but we can also do it intentionally. When we subtly mirror someone, we activate that system in *their* brain too. It's like saying, "I see you. I get you. We're in sync," without uttering a word. The wild part is that people often can't explain why they trust us more. They just do.

Try this:

- Listen to your guest's tone. Are they warm and reflective, or punchy and playful? Match it.
- Use their phrasing, metaphors, and vocabulary. It signals you're in sync. Not all the time. That would be weird. But just enough.

There's a reason we click with some people instantly while others feel like they're on a totally different page. Psychologists call it the similarity-attraction effect. We trust people who seem like us.

There's a brilliant little piece of research by Dr. Paul Zak, a neuroscientist who studied what makes people feel safe enough to open up. He found that when we find something in common with someone – a shared hobby, value, or life experience – our brains release oxytocin, the 'trust hormone' which reduces fear and boosts openness (Zak, 2011). While we tend to assume that we'll either vibe with someone or we won't, the good news is we can create that vibe intentionally.

Try this:

- Show them you've done the work. Have their book nearby, pages dog-eared. Mention a specific quote, not just the title. Have their website up on your screen. That visible prep creates trust, fast.
- Make the first question easy. Ask something they've likely answered before – familiar, not boring. It gives them a chance to relax and feel capable right from the start. You may not even use that answer if it's pre-recorded, but that's not the point. The point is flow.
- Use your face and body. Seriously. Eye contact, nods, warm micro-reactions, they matter. Specifically leaning in and tilting your head to the side makes people feel more interesting than they ever knew they could.
- Reinforce the good vibes. If they give a great answer early on, reflect it back with something like: "That's such a good way to put it..." This tells them: I'm listening, I'm interested, you're safe.

reminded of how brilliant their harmonies are. Then all of a sudden I was in a Finn Brothers deep dive. You know the kind, where hours disappear, and before you know it, you're in the kitchen, attempting high notes you have no business attempting.

Their harmonies really are next-level. So much so that I never quite know if I'm singing the melody or the harmony line; they blend so seamlessly, yet each voice is distinct.

I reckon that's exactly how it should feel when you're hosting. The art of blending or harmonising with your guest is everything: two voices, in tune, in sync, yet distinct. That's rapport.

Once the conversation starts, it's your job to keep it tuned, balanced, and flowing. Researchers call it mutual attunement. I call it *rapport*.

Really, it's about three things:

- Connecting: finding common ground so trust is built quickly.
- Reflecting: mirroring energy naturally, so the guest feels at ease.
- Directing: guiding the conversation subtly so it flows effortlessly.

When you get these right, the conversation does feel a bit like music: fluid, dynamic, and alive. Here's how.

Connect by Tuning

You wouldn't start a duet without tuning your instrument first. Same goes for an interview or meeting. If you want harmony, you need to find a shared frequency. This means we need ways to warm up the conversation, quickly.

The art of blending or harmonising with your guest is everything: two voices, in tune, in sync, yet distinct. That's rapport.

interviews in radio history. It's poignant, raw, and utterly human. But that didn't happen by accident. There is a moment where Sendak reflects on life and death with such aching clarity, explaining his love of life and the world. This was made possible because Gross had done the work. The ritualised prep. The trust-building. The presence. Sendak even wrote to her after the interview to thank her for giving him a space to say things he might not have shared otherwise (Gross, 2012).

So no, Terry Gross doesn't just rely on instinct. She relies on rituals. Tool and systems that allow her to be fully there when it counts.

Next time you're hosting, rather than copying what the pros sound like, copy their systems. Identify their rituals. That's what will make you better each time you host.

- Be Punctual: set rituals so you control time, not the other way around.
- Be Prepared: have tools and processes in place so you can adjust in real-time.
- Be Present: develop grounding techniques to keep you engaged, not distracted.

If you want to feel like a host who's ready for anything, rituals make readiness automatic.

The Rapport Card – Scoring High on Connection in Every Conversation

The other day, I caught the end of a *Crowded House* interview on TV. Even though it was just the last few minutes, I was instantly

Learning from Legends: Terry Gross – The Rituals Behind the Moment

Turns out I'm not the only host who's a ritual fiend. I've got to say I was stoked when I realised that I share this practice with some of the greats. Ahem... Terry Gross level great. You might've heard of her. She's the voice behind NPR's *Fresh Air*, and if you've ever listened to one of her interviews, you'll know exactly what I mean when I say: she's good in-the-moment. But what most people don't see (or hear) is all the stuff Terry does consistently that make her good in the moment. Spoiler: she's does heaps of stuff.

In an interview with the *Columbia Journalism Review*, Gross shared that her preparation starts with total immersion. If she's interviewing a musician, she listens to the full discography. If it's a filmmaker, she watches all the films. Books? Cover to cover, plus reviews. She's not scanning for quotes or dog-earring pages, she's looking for patterns, contradictions, and clues that help her ask the questions no one else does (CJR, 2015).

It's not all homework though. In a *New York Times* piece, Gross revealed one of her rituals is telling guests they can skip any question. No pressure. No awkwardness. Just an invitation to trust the space (NYT, 2015). It sounds small, but it's huge. Because when the guest knows they're safe, they're more likely to go deep.

Then, there's what happens in the moment, which is, of course, backed by rituals. In a 2020 Press Club Institute webinar, Gross talked about her commitment to listening to answers all the way through. That means no looking ahead to the next question. No pre-loading reactions. Just following the thread in real time (Press Club, 2020).

We get to hear the impact of this in her 2011 interview with Maurice Sendak It's widely regarded as one of the most moving

Communication researcher Graham Bodie and his team at Louisiana State University studied what made people seem more engaging and trustworthy. Turns out, it wasn't clever phrasing or dazzling intellect. It was tiny things. Simple things. Things we can turn into rituals.

Their 2015 study found that when people took a single breath before they spoke, or added a deliberate pause, their audience rated them as more charismatic, more credible, and more worth listening to (Bodie et al., 2015). Magic? No. Just the kind of science that makes you go, "Huh. Makes sense."

Try this:

- Start with a circuit-breaker breath. Before you hit record or step on stage, take one deep, deliberate breath in through your nose and out through your mouth. Not a sniffle. Not a sigh. A full stop. It tells your nervous system, "I'm here now."
- Anchor your body to the moment. Feel your feet on the ground. Press your fingertips together. Rest your hands on the table with intention. Tiny physical cues like these bring your focus out of your head and into the room where it needs to be.
- Listen like it's live radio. Don't plan your next line while they're still talking. Listen as if their answer is going straight to air, and *you* have to make the moment work. You want to react to what you heard, not to what you expected to hear.

Presence isn't a mood. It's a decision. And, like any good ritual, the more you practise it, the more natural it becomes.

Try this:

- Audit your setup. Can you find what you need without thinking? Run a quick check: where's your mic? Your notes? Your water? If the nerves hit or something glitches, could you lay your hands on what matters in ten seconds flat?
- Standardise your process. Turn your checklist into a ritual. Whether it's a podcast, a panel, or a team meeting, have a repeatable system for the motions of the show. When the basics become muscle memory, you free up brain space to create moments that matter.
- Test your tools. Never assume the tech will play nice. Check your mic, slides, recording platform, charger, whiteboard markers – even the clicker. Plus stash your essentials nearby: lozenges, water, tissues, paracetamol, whatever your brain or body might need mid-flow. Future you will thank you.

Looking calm isn't enough. Being calm is the goal. That happens when we've already handled those things that might rattle us.

Get Present

Ever watched an interviewer or meeting host who's clearly distracted? You can feel it. It usually happens because they're thinking about their next question instead of listening to the answer, or they're stuck in their own head, worrying about how they're coming across instead of how the conversation is unfolding. Or they're worrying about what's happening in their inbox, online, or outside!

When that happens, it kills the energy. It's as jarring as it is common. Charisma isn't fairy dust. It's not about jazz hands, sparkles, or having a voice that sounds like a warm cinnamon scroll. It's about presence. Being there. For real. Luckily, presence is something we can learn.

- Create a countdown ritual. Use pacing cues to shift into hosting mode. A specific playlist. A hot drink. A ten-minute "door close" rule where you shut out distractions and signal to yourself: *I'm on*. Let the rhythm carry you in.
- Stay time-aware, not time-ruled. Glance at the clock, don't stare at it. Use time as a gentle guide, not a pressure point. Think of it like a lighthouse: steady in the background, there if you need it.

Use time to support you, instead of pushing you.

Be Prepared

Preparation isn't just about knowing what we'll say. It's about having the right tools, in the right place, so when things go sideways (and they will), we will *still* know what to say. Yep, this is the stuff of an orienteer.

Make sure you pack your backpack with your version of a compass, a map, and snacks long before your 'thing' starts. While you're packing, make sure the tools aren't just piled in, but have their own place so you can grab them quickly when you need them.

Harvard behavioural researcher Francesca Gino, part psychologist, part workplace wizard, discovered something beautifully obvious: when people prepare their tools in the same, consistent way before high-pressure moments, their brains stay fresher for longer. In her 2015 study, Gino found that this ritualised setup reduced mental fatigue and decision overload (Gino et al., 2015). It's like KonMari for your cognition, everything in its place, so your mind can be in the moment.

Another way to think about it is, the more automatic your setup is, the more brainpower you have left for the actual conversation.

Here are three types of rituals that I recommend all hosts develop to help stay calm, confident, and in control, no matter what's thrown at you.

Be Punctual

Have you noticed that a great host is never rushing? Never scrambling. Never playing catch-up. Why? Because they are just naturally brilliant? Maybe. But it's more likely because they have punctuality rituals that create a buffer, keeping them ahead of time, rather than racing it. While it feels like we should just start earlier, I've learned it's more about starting with intention.

Sabine Häfner and her team at the University of Konstanz explored the stress levels of people who worked with fixed start times versus those who worked to looming deadlines. The outcome? Those with a defined start time experienced less stress, more focus, and better adaptability when plans changed (Häfner et al., 2014). Translation: start on purpose.

Now, I'm sure there are many great hosts out there who'll swear by the last-minute scramble, and sure, maybe I'm just seeing what I want to see, but if there is research that says a defined start time helps us show up calm, clear, and in control, I'm listening. It's worth reiterating that the goal is about *being on* time, it's about *feeling ready* in time.

Try this:

- Set a start time for your prep, not just your show or event. Don't rely on the deadline (or dreadline, as I used to call them). Choose an exact time when you'll *start* preparing. Not "sometime before the event," but "10:30am sharp." When you know when the warm-up starts, the panic fades.

Why rely on willpower or
luck when you can rely
on systems?

To an outsider, these rituals were invisible (perhaps, not so invisible to my producers and colleagues...). To me they were the reason I could be fully present on-air without feeling frantic. Plus, if something ever went wrong, I'd add a new ritual to help me be ready for it next time. From the way I set up my notes to how I walked in and out of the studio, it was all designed to take the stress out of hosting. Did I become a little superstitious about these rituals by the end? Maybe. However, they were brought into being because I knew that when things went wrong (and they always do in live situations), my rituals would catch me.

Why Hosts Need Rituals

Hosting is unpredictable. Guests go rogue. Tech fails. An audience member asks a question that throws everything out. When that happens, which it will, you don't want to be scrambling. Why rely on willpower or luck, when you can rely on systems?

"We do not rise to the level of our goals;
we fall to the level of our systems."

– James Clear, *Atomic Habits*, 2018

A well-designed ritual isn't just a habit, it's your built-in backup plan. It creates readiness. It means when the unexpected happens, you don't freeze, flail, or fill the silence with waffle. You just know what to do next. If you look at top athletes, musicians, and performers, you'll notice they all have pre-game/gig rituals that help them get into the right mindset before they step into the spotlight. Hosting is no different.

During 75

While this might sound like an arbitrary deadline, it was an intentional strategy. Having only an hour to prepare the words stopped me from overthinking my stories and scripts. It kept me fresh, so I didn't get too locked into ideas and could respond naturally to what unfolded during the show. Basically, it stopped me from overcooking it. It was my way of creating a structured but flexible mindset that kept me ready without feeling over-rehearsed. This ritual made me *me* when the mic was on.

Then, 15 minutes before the show, I'd print my scripts, staple them in order (of appearance), and stack them neatly on my desk. I'd then go into the studio and set it up the same way every time, in the same order every time; I'd adjust my mic and put up certain faders to the top, others halfway, and leave others down (yep, that's a thing). I'd place scripts in a certain spot, in a certain order. I'd open computer programs and websites one by one, then move my 'cart stacks' to the on-air program, and double check their order, all before making sure my pen (and back-up pen) was exactly where I needed it.

I'd do all this, the same way, every time. Scripts. Stack. Mic. Faders. Programs. Cart stacks. Pen. It became muscle memory.

During the show, I had plenty of rituals too. I'd cross things off my rundown as a way to track time. I'd get up and welcome guests in and then get up and see them out as a way to move my body and keep my energy up. I'd write down the next three segments in order to help me commit them to memory and save me from getting lost after a tough interview. I had a list of extra ideas close by at all times in case the show went sideways, I always had something interesting to move on to.

And after the show? I'd close the computer programs down in the same order, staple my notes together, file them away, and finalise all other jobs, so the day felt complete, not chaotic.

"Shhhiiiiiiiittttttt."

Hmmmm. Yep. Not my best work.

This chapter is about making hosting *work* in the moment, no matter what's thrown your way. Here's what we'll cover:

- The Rituals: the small, intentional habits that keep you in control when everything else feels out of control.
- The Rapport Card: how to connect with guests quickly and get them to open up.
- The Route: get to know my Question Compass™, the ultimate tool for navigating interviews.

Let's get into it.

The Rituals – The Secret to Feeling Ready, Every Time

I never thought of myself as a rituals person. I used to call them routines. Rituals sounded a bit too woo woo for me. But over time, I realised there's a difference (and that I'm totally a rituals person).

A routine is something you do without much thought, like brushing your teeth. A ritual is something you do with intention; a deliberate practice that helps you feel ready. As it turns out, I have a lot of rituals.

Back when I was working in radio, I had a set process I'd follow before every show. Not just in the moments before I turned on the mic, but from at least an hour before until an hour after my show.

Let's start with the first one. I convinced myself I didn't need to think about my show prep until exactly one hour before the show.

A ritual is something you do with intention; a deliberate practice that helps you feel ready.

The first happened when I was set up for an outside broadcast at Beauty Point in Tasmania. We were there to cover something significant — a navy ship arrival, or a new aquaculture facility, or both — I can't quite remember. Everything was running smoothly until it wasn't. Ten minutes before I was supposed to go on air, we lost connection.

My technical producer was scrambling to troubleshoot, trying every possible fix, but nothing was working. We had another producer back in the studio on standby to play a song, giving us more time to figure it out. But this wasn't ideal, what we needed was a show. In the world of live broadcasts, this is up there with the worst scenario you could get. Yet, somehow, I didn't panic.

Instead, I watched the time closely but focused more on chatting with the person I was about to interview, keeping them relaxed, even as I knew the seconds were slipping away. I checked the news feed, the weather, and my notes. I had one eye on my producer, one on my guest, and some other extra eye on the clock.

Then, with no more than two seconds to spare, my producer gave me a nod. We'd reconnected. I took a breath, played my opening sting, and started the show as if nothing had happened. The audience never knew. The guests weren't panicked. The show went on. It was a win.

That day, in that moment, I felt the payoff of my carefully crafted instincts and tools. Another time, things didn't go quite so smoothly.

I was hosting *The Country Hour* for the first time. I'd carefully written and was delivering my one-minute intro before crossing to the national news feed. I lifted the fader, and... nothing. I tried another... still nothing. I put them all up... crickets. The switching was wrong. No news. No feed. Just me and my mic. And into that mic I let out a perfectly clear, very audible, very long:

During

Make Hosting Feel Effortless

You've set the foundations. You've calibrated, curated, and prepared. The conversation's primed, the guests are poised, and the mic is hot. But preparation only gets you so far.

Once you're live, whether it's a podcast, a panel, or a planning meeting, it's all about how you move in the moment. The space can shift. The energy can dip. Sometimes the air can feel thick; occasionally, it vanishes altogether, and it feels like you can't breathe. This is why we can't rely on preparation alone.

Now it's about reading the room and, if needed, rewiring the rhythm in real time. It's about being present enough to respond, prepared enough to pivot, structured enough to create flow. It's about The Orienteering Bat. The Great Toast. The [insert your own metaphor here].

Dealing with the Moment

I remember clearly two instances where I had to deal with the moment. One good, one not so good, both great learning experiences.

- **The Preparation**: you've learned how to read and tune the three invisible forces — the situation, the relationships, and the vibe — to help your guest shine and your audience lean in.

This is what stops you from becoming a dry host who drains the energy, or a burnt one who scripts the soul out of it. You're becoming the host people trust to hold space, steer the conversation, and make every moment feel like it matters.

However, we're not even halfway yet. Once the mic's on, the real fun begins (insert awkward and slightly evil laugh). Up next? The moment-by-moment craft of hosting live. How to listen, react, and guide a conversation that sticks.

And when he finally shouted, "Let's jump!" we didn't need to ask how high. We already knew. And that, my friends, is the job of a host (actually, let's call it a gig so we can channel some of those rockstar vibes!)

Hosting isn't about bringing the energy, it's about preparing to *co-create* one. While you don't need to be a rockstar to pull this off, you *do* need to know what kind of room you're walking into and what kind of energy you want to leave behind.

Before You Start, Set the Stage and Set Yourself

If I can draw your attention back to the most common question I used to get as a radio host, "What time do you start work?" The answer is: long enough before the show goes live to do all of the above. Not the glamorous bits people see; the effortless questions, the well-timed laughs, the perfectly framed guest reactions. But the bits before that. The bits that make all those other bits possible. The *actual* stuff. The prep work that moves you up the host ladder, moving you further away from making it up and closer to making it matter.

Here's what you've now got in your kit:

- **The Calibration**: you know how to align the guest, the audience, and the purpose so the whole thing clicks.
- **The Curation**: you're collecting, sorting, and shaping ideas like a pro, so you're never stuck making small talk when the moment calls for depth.

Learning from Legends: Sam Hales – What I Learned from a Frontman at the Back of the Forth Pub

We've all heard of the pub test. You know the one: would this idea, policy, or person get a tick of approval during a chat at your local? It's a shorthand for checking if an idea is in tune with real people, in a real place. It's a great litmus test for how something *lands*. But the best test I've ever seen at a pub was a completely different kind of test, yet it did a similar job. Just better.

Not long ago, I found myself at the pub in the tiny Tasmanian town of Forth, right in the middle of winter. From the outside, the Forth Pub looks like your classic country hotel, but step through the back door, and it reveals itself as one of Australia's most iconic live music venues. Out the back sits a purpose-built shed for live music, and that night, it was packed. Fifteen hundred of us, shoulder to shoulder, waiting to see the Australian band *The Jungle Giants*.

Now, I've been to my fair share of gigs, but what lead singer Sam Hales did that night has stuck with me ever since. As he stepped onto the stage, he grabbed the mic and called out, "How are you all doing?" – a standard frontman move. But what he did next was far from standard. He didn't move on or dive into the first song. He paused. He walked the stage. He looked around. He crouched down. Made eye contact. He listened.

Then he said, "Yeah, I can feel that." He wasn't assuming we were ready to match his energy. It was as though he was testing the vibe, instead of demanding it. But it was more than that; he was tuning his energy to ours.

Over the next 20 minutes, he kept checking in, he kept tuning. Between songs he'd crouch again, scan the room, smile, soften, adjust. He warmed us up slowly, intentionally, reading the room before raising the roof.

Responding to the vibe is one thing (which we'll dive into deeper in the next section), but planning for it is another. So, for now, prep like the vibe it matters. Because it does.

Try this:

- Test the vibe before you start. We do this through research. Know what's going on in the room (if it's an event or meeting), in the world (if it's a broadcast or podcast), and with your guest (if it's a conversation). Preparing for the overarching 'mood' and crafting ways to acknowledge it is what lets you meet people where they are, rather than where you want them to be.

- Choose where you want the vibe to land. Once you know where they are, decide where you want to take them. Should they feel calm? Curious? Energised? Uplifted? Set that intention early, and think about how you'll signal it through tone, tempo, posture, humour, or even the way you walk into the space. Energy is contagious. Make yours deliberate.

- Plan to reset when it matters. Shifting the vibe well isn't a reaction; it's an intention. Sometimes, you'll need to change pace from deep reflection to fast momentum. Other times, you'll feel attention drifting and know it's time to wake the room up. Plan for these resets. Have stories, questions, props, phrases, pauses, or even music ready to shift the feeling and bring people with you, not just at the start, but throughout.

- Connection: This current creates warmth, trust, and safety. But left unchecked, it can slow things down or soften the edges too much.
- Curiosity: This is a current that can open up new thinking and invite reflection. But without direction, it can scatter attention or dilute the message.

These aren't 'good' or 'bad' states. They're just signals. The key is noticing which one is present and choosing how to respond. Once we've assessed the current, we can use our 'presence' to match it and then move it. I've found the best way to do this is by adjusting our mannerisms, our momentum, and our mojo.

Mannerisms are the small signals we send before we say a word. How we smile, gesture, move through the space, tilt our head while listening, breathe between points, or hold a gaze just long enough to show someone we're with them. Even a dropped or lifted shoulder can match or shift the tone.

Momentum is the speed and shape of how we speak or steer the conversation. Sometimes it's tight, fast, and focused. Other times it's meandering, slow, and reflective. We can hold a pause to stretch a moment, or pick up pace to drive it forward.

And then there's mojo. That's our unique communication spark and is often the thing that wakes people up. It might be a flash of wit, a moment of calm, a well-timed story, a curious question, or a line that cuts through the noise.

When we adjust these three things with intention, we're able to assess the energy, match it, and move it where it needs to go. It lets us tune the energy, rather than force it.

and it's as contagious as a yawn (and unless you're hosting a restorative yoga retreat, yawning is not the vibe you're hoping for). Too often, I see hosts preparing for how the moment will sound, yet forget to prepare for how the moment might *feel*. When we skip this step, the tone gets away from us. Meetings feel flat, conversations feel forced, and audiences drift off. It's usually not because the content is wrong, but because the energy didn't carry it. That's why prepping for the vibe matters.

Psychologist Daniel Goleman, who brought emotional intelligence into the mainstream, calls this social intelligence: your ability to pick up emotional cues and respond in a way that builds trust (Goleman, 2006). This isn't about being warm and fuzzy, it's about learning to read those cues that help you know when to pause, pivot, or go deep.

So, how do we do it? Light some incense and chant affirmations? Sure! Give it a go if you like; however, I reckon a more useful first step is to get a sense of the energy we're walking into and make a plan for how we'll manage it. Only then will we know if we need the incense and affirmations on standby.

Every room carries an emotional current. You'll often recognise one of the following four currents in a space and, like a battery, each one comes with a positive and negative charge:

- Clarity: This current helps people focus and tune in. But overdo it, and it can feel sharp, cold, or rigid, like there's no room to move.
- Charge: This current can show up as excitement and urgency, but also as anger or overwhelm if it's too intense.

Some people can smell rain.
Good hosts can smell the
vibe. They're not magic.
They're just paying attention.

that helps them reflect? Get clear on what *they* need, not just what *you* prefer.

- The first message sets the tone. Long before the mic goes live, you're already shaping how safe, seen, and supported your guest feels.
  - If they're new to this, let them know what to expect. If it's pre-recorded, say so. If it's live, reassure them you're ready to catch them. Start teasing out a few stories and gently point to what might really land with your audience and why.
  - If they're nervous about the tech, give them time to test. Let them know you'll fill the space if anything glitches, that nothing's too silly to ask, and that you've got them.
  - If they're a seasoned pro, be clear about what kind of conversation you're aiming for. Gently guide them on what your audience might need from them this time around.
- Test for trust gaps. Before you kick off, look for tension in the dynamic. Nerves from the guest? Hesitation in the room? Acknowledge it. Find common ground. Share something small and human to level the playing field.

The Vibe

You know that moment when you walk into a room and something's... off? No one says anything, but everyone *feels* it. That's the vibe. Some people can smell rain. Good hosts can smell the vibe. They're not magic. They're just paying attention.

The energy in the room builds before words are spoken and lingers long after. It shapes what people hear, how they interpret it, and whether they'll act. It's the emotional tone behind the moment,

So, if you're waiting 'til the red light starts blinking to try and make your guest feel safe, you're already too late.

That feeling of safety needs to start from the very first interaction. An email. A phone call. A DM. A pre-interview chat. Every touchpoint sets a tone. That tone is often shaped by the role you're playing, even if you don't realise you're playing one. Let me explain.

While we know that hosting isn't about playing the starring role, what many forget is that it's not even about playing a single role. It's about playing the right role for that moment.

Sometimes, we need to show up as the Anchor – quiet, grounded, and reflective. We help steady the space by thinking before we speak and slowing the moment down.

Sometimes, we're the Adventurer – asking curious, open questions that take the conversation somewhere new. Other times, we step in as the Amplifier – lifting the energy, echoing important points, and helping others feel seen and heard. Sometimes, we're the Advocate – sharing a clear, thoughtful perspective that cuts through the noise and helps people make sense of what matters. When we can pick the right role for the right moment, people feel safer. It's not about playing a character, it's about making a choice about which part of you is needed in that moment. It's that choice that shapes how open people are when speaking, listening, contributing, and caring.

Even if our guests are terrified of the microphone, let's make sure they're not terrified of us, eh?

Try this:
- Ask: Who am I to this person right now? Am I the anchor they'll lean on? The hype person who lifts them? The mirror

- Identify the levers you can adjust mid-flow. When the situation shifts, what can you tweak? The seating? The focus? The pace? The structure? Maybe it's about adding a cup of tea. That was enough for Enid.

The Relationships

Every time we host, we're stepping into a relationship. Or rather, three of them:

- You and your guest.
- You and your audience.
- Your guest and your audience.

This three-way is powered by trust. Trust doesn't happen by accident; it happens because of who you choose to *be*, well before the formal conversation begins.

Psychologist Carl Rogers was one of the first to show that people open up more when they feel accepted, heard, and understood (Rogers, 1957). He called it *unconditional positive regard*, which is a fancy term for what happens when we show up with generosity. Fast-forward a few decades, and Amy Edmondson gave us the concept of *psychological safety*, a shared sense that it's safe to speak, share, or ask questions without being shut down (Edmondson, 1999). And – spoiler – psychological safety doesn't start with rules. It starts with interactions. Especially those of the host.

If you think the best time to start thinking about safety is when the microphone turns on... have you met a microphone?! Microphones are terrifying for most people. They're like truth serum crossed with a spotlight. For most people, speaking in public ranks somewhere between skydiving and being chased by a shark while skydiving.

Creating the right environment for good conversations takes prep: researching the people, knowing the context, anticipating what might shift, and testing the tools you'll need to re-tune the space when it does.

Try this:

- Do your research. Properly. Don't just scan the Wikipedia bio or skim the company's 'About' page. Get your boots in the back paddock. Listen to old interviews, read past reports, dig up last year's conference agendas, and find the lesser-known podcast episode. The goal is to get your brain into *their* world, so you can meet them where they actually are, not where Google says they are.

- Sit where they'll sit. Literally. Plonk yourself in the chair your guest or audience will use. What does it feel like? Are they exposed? On display? Too far from the action? Too far *in* it? You can't create safety if you don't understand the vantage point.

- Clear the clutter. Visual noise creates mental noise. A chaotic space signals a chaotic experience. Tidy the table. Straighten the chairs. Remove distractions. Make the space feel cared for. When the environment looks like it matters, people are more likely to believe that they do too.

- Check the shape of the space. Is it a boardroom built for decisions, or a circle built for contribution? Is it open and relaxed, or rigid and performative? The geometry of the room says something before you even speak. Make sure what it's saying matches the conversation you're trying to have.

The Situation

This isn't just about chairs and lighting (though, yes, those matter). The situation is the context and conditions we're operating within. It shapes how people show up and how they behave. What's the background here? What's the history? What do some people know that others don't? Is the space set for hierarchy or contribution? Is it chaotic or calm? Open or closed? Predictable or volatile?

Great hosts consider all of these questions before anything goes live. It's what allows us to create a space that encourages connection once the mic is on. It's about noticing where the power is sitting, how permission is being signalled, and what kind of pace the moment needs.

Environmental psychologists have been onto this for years. Back in 1974, Albert Mehrabian and James A. Russell found that our surroundings don't just influence how we feel, they *shape how we behave* (Mehrabian and Russell, 1974). They built a model (fancy term: Stimulus – Organism – Response) showing that when we step into a space, we're not just taking in the lighting or the furniture, we're subconsciously deciding how to act. Is it safe here? Am I on display? Can I relax? The answers to those questions affect whether someone leans in or shuts down.

Mehrabian and Russell identified three key emotional responses: pleasure (how comfortable it feels), arousal (how stimulating it is), and dominance (how much control we feel in that space). So, if the room feels warm, welcoming, and calm, people open up. If it's cold, loud, or awkward — like sitting on a swivel stool under a fluoro light — they clam up. And yes, this absolutely applies to Zoom rooms, too. When we shape the space as hosts, it's about much more than rearranging the chairs; it's about setting the emotional tone for the entire conversation.

Not because the mic was too sensitive but because we were all holding our breath, waiting for her next line.

As we walked down the hallway afterwards, me in front, Enid following behind, I was giving the usual wrap-up — when to listen, how to tune in, the standard spiel – when we reached the end and I turned to thank her, I'll never forget what happened next. Enid looked at me and said, "I am pretty interesting, aren't I?"

Yes, Enid. Yes, you are.

Over my career, I've come to realise that most people are like Enid. There are so incredibly interesting, but just need someone to remind them.

That's how I came up with something I call The Enid Process. It's how we set the conditions that let the 'interesting' come out of one person and land with another. It's how we remind people they're worth listening to and get the audience to believe it too.

This part of hosting is such an important and unique skill that it's become the foundation for my broader body of work called **Shift the Signal**™. It's about managing three invisible dynamics that determine whether people connect or check out.

That management starts way *before* the room fills, the mic turns on, or the spotlight hits. While part of your preparation needs to be about researching the topics, making notes, and checking the tech, the first bit is about the dynamics.

Before anything begins, we want to tune into three things:

- The situation we're walking into.
- The relationships we're about to be in.
- The vibe we're creating (or inheriting).

Let's break them down.

sense. We're preparing to disrupt *boring* people and *bored* people. Yep, and it's a big part of the gig.

I have a very firm belief that no one is boring. They've usually just forgotten what makes them interesting and it's our job, as hosts, to remind them.

Likewise, people aren't bored because the topic's dull. They're bored because no one's made them care, yet. That is also our job.

I still remember the day I learned this was my job. It was a penny-dropping moment (pun intentional) on a cold Tasmanian morning in a tiny town called Chudleigh, while I was working for ABC Radio.

These were my favourite days. Our program did multiple out-side broadcasts a month, often multiple in a week. My producer, Andrea and I developed a bit of a routine – we'd turn up in a town early, hit the post office or butcher for local intel, and start knocking on doors to find good yarns.

At 8:30am that particular morning, I knocked on one of those doors. A woman in her late seventies answered, called Enid. Enid seemed friendly, but pretty cautious. "Hi," I said, "I'm Penny from the ABC. We're broadcasting from down the road this afternoon. Any chance I could interview you about your life here in Chudleigh?"

Quick as a flash, she said, "Why would you want to interview me? I've got nothing interesting to say." I'd heard this exact line hundreds of times before, so I brushed it aside and suggested we have a cup of tea and see what we could learn. We made tea. We chatted. And 30 minutes later, Andrea and I were sitting in stunned silence listening to Enid's stories. Stories of family, change, resilience, humour, all told with a sharp wit and a warm heart.

When I listened back to the tape later, I noticed that every time Enid paused, I could hear the fridge humming in the background.

In *The Guardian* (Cain, 2022), Glass said the best stories come from staffers who get "obsessed with something and want to know everything about it." They collect weird angles, half-finished thoughts, strange characters, and slowly build a show from the inside out. It's less like writing and more like sifting – curating not just what's good, but what *fits*.

Importantly, he says, the moment that makes it land isn't the big twist or the fancy production. It's meaning. In *The Guardian*, Glass explains a story only sticks if "somebody has to have a thought about what it means." It doesn't need to be deep, but it has to connect. That little reflection, that spark of resonance, is what makes a pile of stories into a curated *show*.

We can't rely on inspiration to embody us in the moment. As hosts, we need a system to curate ideas *before* we need them.

- Break the algorithm: gather new ideas from unexpected places.
- Filter the fluff: cut what doesn't serve the conversation.
- Make it interesting: frame and deliver ideas in a way that makes it matter to them (the audience).

This is the hidden work. The behind-the-scenes craft that makes the front-of-scenes better.

The Preparation – Tuning the Situation, Relationship, and Vibe

Why Preparation Matters

As hosts, we're preparing to disrupt. But not in the tech-bro reckons our collective attention crisis is less about discipline and more about design. He rightly explains that the world is built to distract us. Which means when we *do* manage to hold someone's attention, it's a minor miracle! And as a host we are in the business of miracles.

Learning how to get and keep attention is crucial. It's all about making it matter *to them*.

Try this:
- Surprise: *Get attention.* Start with something unexpected – a standout fact, a contradiction, a bold statement.
- Suspense: *Keep attention.* Keep people leaning in by creating tension, curiosity, or an open loop. Don't rush the payoff.
- Insight: *Extend attention.* Leave them with a 'Huh!' moment, something they'll repeat at dinner tonight.

Learning from Legends: Ira Glass – It's Not a Story Until It Means Something

If there were a Mount Rushmore of podcast hosts, Ira Glass would be chiselled in granite, headphones and all. But the thing that makes his long running radio show and podcast *This American Life* so good isn't just his now iconic voice, it's the ruthless way he curates content.

Glass has talked often about the show's process, and – spoiler – it's scary. In a Columbia University lecture (Glass, 2018), he said, "Most stories we try, die in the process." His team gets heaps of pitches every week, and most of them don't make it past the first few steps. Why? Because a good idea isn't enough. They need structure. Surprise. Something that matters.

- Rank them by impact. Ask yourself: "Which of these will land hardest with this audience, right now?" Be honest. What's timely? What's useful? What will actually shift thinking?
- Cut what's nice but unnecessary. If it's just there to fill space or make you sound smart, it can go. Less noise, more signal.

Filtering ideas before you bring them to others makes you better, makes the conversation better, makes the impact better. It just makes everything better.

Make It Interesting

Even the best idea won't land unless we know how to deliver it (see: Great Toast Theory). This is where we need to maintain our creativity and not get stuck in our default settings. We need to be relentless in our efforts to surprise people, keep them curious, and spotlight something to take away.

Sadly, humans officially have a shorter attention span than goldfish (McSpadden, 2015). Actually, it's not official. I read an article that told me the research methods of this study have been questioned (plus measuring a goldfish's attention span is a weird flex to begin with), but honestly, that's all I can tell you. Because by the time I got to that part of the article that told me why the methods were questioned, I'd got bored. And that, my friends, is the point.

As a host, it's often our job to help make other people's content interesting, and that takes some thought. We need to have thought about how we will get people hooked from the get-go, rather than hoping the message will find its feet halfway through. It's worth remembering that audiences don't stick around for the 'good bit.' If it gets boring, they're gone. Focus, stolen.

Speaking of which, Johan Hari, in his book *Stolen Focus* (2022),

As a host, it's often our job to help make other people's content interesting.

split-second choice: cull, keep, or sell. Some were moved on. Some stayed. Some weren't ready... yet.

Same goes for hosting. We've got to sort ideas quickly and ruthlessly.

Before an idea makes it through your drafting gate, ask:

- Is it reliable? Can I trust this?
- Is it relevant? Does it serve my audience?
- Is it relatable? Will people connect with it?

I know it feels tough, but we can't keep all our ideas. We're an ideas farm, not an ideas shelter. Plus, our brain doesn't love clutter. Back in the late '80s, Australian educational psychologist John Sweller came up with something called Cognitive Load Theory, and it's still one of the most important ideas for anyone trying to get a message to stick. Sweller (1988) found that when we throw too much information at people, their brains get overwhelmed. The excess detail doesn't help but blocks learning. It's like trying to read a great book while someone's vacuuming next to your head.

When people show up to listen, watch, or be part of a conversation, they're giving us their time and attention – arguably the two most valuable things they can share with us. They don't have unlimited headspace and they trust us to bring them what's worth hearing, not half-baked ideas or filler content. Respect that.

Try this:
- Before a meeting or interview, jot down five key ideas you want to explore. Not word-for-word scripts, just the core messages or topics that align with the show.

our brain is more flexible, our questions get sharper, our framing gets clearer, and our conversations land better. We stop serving up the same predictable ideas and start creating moments that make people think, laugh, or say, "I've never thought of it that way before." And honestly, if you can get your audience to think that, your job is done. It's the most powerful thought you can elicit. It means they weren't just listening, they were shifting. Mic. Drop.

Try this:

- Follow five new voices on social media each week. Bonus points if you don't agree with them. The goal isn't to argue, it's to stretch your feed beyond the echo chamber.
- Listen to a podcast from a totally different industry. Arts, sport, science, or even farming, it doesn't matter. Look for ideas you can borrow, shape, or apply in your own way.
- Start a conversation outside your usual circle. Ask someone in a different field, "What's the big issue in your workplace this week?" You'll be surprised by what insights you pick up when you tune into a different frequency.

When it comes to your ideas, think like a farmer. Go out and check the back paddocks. The best way to surprise your audience is to surprise yourself first.

Filter the Fluff

Collecting is the fun part. But I caution you, dear reader: we live in a world designed to deceive and influence us, if you can believe it. Not all ideas deserve a seat at the table. We have to do more than collect them, we need to filter them.

Before Dad let the sheep through the drafting gate, he had a

A great host is always searching for fresh ideas in unexpected places. Breaking out of our content bubble rewires our brain.

They build a system – they've got workdogs, sheep yards, ear tags, a skinny yard called a 'race' with a three-way gate at the end – so when it's time to sort, they can make fast, clear decisions about where each sheep belongs.

Great hosts do the same thing with ideas. They're always drafting – collecting, sorting, filtering – so when the mic turns on, they've already done the thinking and have the right ideas ready to go.

It's time to learn how to be more like a farmer.

Break the Algorithm

One of the biggest challenges in hosting is learning how to *round up* ideas. Just like a farmer knows their sheep won't simply wander into the yards, we can't expect ideas to gather themselves. We need to head out to the back paddocks and bring them in.

However, most of us don't. We live inside our own personal algorithms, scrolling through the same familiar feeds, seeing things we already agree with, hearing ideas we've heard a hundred times before and then we wonder why nothing feels fresh.

That's a massive risk when we're hosting. Because if we're not actively chasing down new perspectives, we're not actively shaping new conversations. We end up recycling the same examples, the same questions, and the same lukewarm hot takes that our audience has already heard. A great host is always searching for fresh ideas in unexpected places.

Breaking out of our content bubble rewires our brain. Seriously. Researchers Spiro and Jehng (1990) found that when we're exposed to a wider mix of ideas, stories, and viewpoints, we build something called cognitive flexibility. Who doesn't want that?! This means having the mental agility to shift gears, see things from different angles, and adapt on the fly. That's gold for hosts. When

What I love most is how he trusts the room. He knows that real moments don't come from perfect scripting, but from the calibration between the three moving parts.

That's hosting. Know your mix. Toss the prompt. Trust the couch.

Get Calibrated

Before you host your next event, meeting, or podcast:

- Calibrate the conversation: you, your guest, and your audience.
- Bridge the knowledge gap: meet your audience where they are.
- Pick the right voices: choose guests who inform *and* engage.

When you *calibrate first*, everything else will flow.

The Curation – How to Find and Sort Ideas Before You Need Them

Why Curation Matters

I grew up on a sheep, cattle and cropping farm, and one of my strongest memories is watching Dad draft sheep. It's mesmerising. If you've never seen it, drafting is how farmers separate sheep into groups: lambs from ewes, big from small, the keepers from the sellers. It's fast, it's precise, it's an art. It's also integral to the whole sheep farming operation.

I've come to realise that drafting sheep is very similar to drafting ideas. A good farmer doesn't stand in a paddock, hoping the right sheep will wander into the right yard when the truck arrives.

Learning from Legends: Graham Norton – Welcome to the Couch: Where Chaos Is Calibrated

Every time I watch *The Graham Norton Show*, I find myself thinking the same thing: How does he pull this off? A couch full of A-listers, half a bottle of pinot gris down, everyone talking over each other, and somehow it still feels like magic. It looks chaotic, but behind the scenes, I reckon Graham Norton is a master of calibration.

Graham Norton seems to host in a way that releases control rather than holding it. The result is a delight to watch. He told *The New Yorker* that the job of a host is "quite a confusing one" because it starts with the spotlight on you, but then quickly flips. "It's your job to elevate [the guests] ... to make them funnier, more famous, more interesting than they might otherwise be." He talks about his real role as being like "A comedy butler" (Russell, 2025). Norton has mastered this in such a way that what looks like effortless fun is actually finely tuned design.

My favourite thing I've learned reading about and watching the Graham Norton show is the prep. It's deep! Apparently (I can't remember where I read this, so it could be fabricated, but still the point is valid), Norton's team scours guest bios looking for any overlap between them – same school, shared ex, surprise fandom – anything that might make a spontaneous spark fly once they hit the couch. I love this so much because once you know this, you see what it does on the show. Rather than asking tightly scripted questions, Norton trusts the work he and the team have done to calibrate before the show. He then throws out prompts and watches what happens. "Those are my favourite nights, when the couch kind of takes off and I'm just literally sat there," he shared (Russell, 2025).

stellar guest. But being brilliant at something doesn't always translate into being great at explaining it, especially to people outside their world.

Deimen and Szalay (2019) explored this in a study on expert communication. They found that subject-matter experts often struggle to connect with general audiences because they forget to adapt their language, unpack their assumptions, or step out of their insider bubble. In other words: the *Curse of Knowledge* strikes again.

And it's not just experts. Celebrities, comedians, and sports stars might light up a room in their domain, but that doesn't guarantee they'll be a great guest. Sometimes they are and it's amazing, but it's worth remembering that fame, titles, and TED Talks don't always equal the right fit. You're looking for resonance, not just credentials.

In theatre, a *triple threat* is someone who can sing, dance, *and* act. In hosting, our triple threat is a guest who is informed, in-tune, *and* interesting. Before you book anyone, you want to run them through the Triple Threat Guest Audit.

Try this:

When you assess potential guests, panellists, or speaker, make sure they tick these boxes as a very minimum:

- Informed: Do they know their stuff? Are they credible? You don't want to have to fact check them later.
- In-Tune: Can they relate to your audience in a way that connects? When a guest is in-tune it's impossible for them to be tone-deaf. Let's not get cancelled, eh?
- Interesting: Are they willing to go beyond facts and into a real conversation, vulnerability and stories? We're looking for guests who can make their message mean something.

Someone who may seem like the best guest *on paper* isn't always the best guest *in conversation.*

Try this:

Use a three-sentence calibration tool to shape your next intro:
- What does my audience already know? Start with something familiar and clear.
- What don't they know but need to? Introduce a *knowledge gap* to spark curiosity.
- Why does it matter? Show them the pay off. Tell them what they'll get if they stick with you.

(This structure works for almost any introduction, but be mindful not to become formulaic. Because, ah, boring.)

When we meet people where they are, they'll follow us (almost) anywhere.

Choosing the Right Guest (or Partner)

Just because someone is an expert doesn't mean they're an expert guest. Mum thought an architect would be great at Pictionary, but incredible drawing skills don't equal effective and fast communication.

Hosting is the same. Someone who may seem like the best guest *on paper* isn't always the best guest *in conversation*. To bring in yet another analogy, the perfect guest is like assembling the ultimate sandwich. Sure, that artisanal cheese (a.k.a. the renowned expert) looks impressive, but if it doesn't mesh with the other ingredients, your sandwich (or show) might end up a soggy mess. It's tempting to think that just because someone is a big cheese in their field (pun not only intended but crafted), they'll automatically be a

The Curse of Knowledge was first described by economists Colin Camerer, George Loewenstein, and Martin Weber in 1989. But the most famous example of it comes from a 1990 study by Elizabeth Newton at Stanford. In her now-famous study, Elizabeth Newton (1990) showed how people wildly overestimate what others will understand.

Participants played a simple game:

- One group were *tappers*, who tapped out well-known songs.
- The other group were *guessers*, who had to identify the tune.

The *tappers* predicted the *guessers* would guess the song correctly about 50% of the time. But in reality, the *guessers* only got it right 2.5% of the time. Hopeless? Nah, the tappers were cursed by knowledge.

The tappers could hear the melody in their head, but the listeners only heard tapping.

The same goes for hosts. We often assume people are following along because *we* know what we mean. But chances are, they're a few steps behind, wondering why this matters and where it's going. We think it's implied, but we didn't give them enough explicit information for them to connect the dots... or the taps. We skipped the context. We didn't show them what's in it for them. Without that, they're not with us. To bring people with us, we've got to bring them *into* it first.

Try this:

Before you step into hosting mode, ask:
- How do I want the audience to *feel*?
- What do I want them to *know*?
- What do I want them to *do*?
- And how can my guest and I help make that happen?

Answer those four, and you'll be aligned before you've even opened your mouth.

Bringing Your Audience with You

It's easy to stay inside our own heads with everything we know and care about. It's much harder to climb into someone else's. But that's the job. One of the biggest traps is something called The Curse of Knowledge. While it sounds like something that would happen in a *Harry Potter* novel, it's actually a cognitive bias that happens in our heads! It makes us terrible at recognising what other people do or don't know. Put simply, once we know something, it's almost impossible to remember what it was like to not know that thing. What now seems obvious to us, isn't obvious to others. At all.

If we go back to the Pictionary example, our drawing makes perfect sense to us. Yet our partner can't seem to guess it, so what do we do? We draw a circle around the thing we've drawn. If they still can't get it? We draw arrows pointing to it. And if they *still* can't get it? We start ribbing them for being hopeless when really, we're the ones who drew a squiggle and expected genius. Because *we* can see it. We've forgotten what it's like to be looking at it with no context.

It's easy to stay inside our own heads with everything we know and care about. It's much harder to climb into someone else's. But that's the job.

- Get the guest-fit right: choose people who add real value, not just a fancy bio.

Let's break these down.

Seeing the Whole Picture

Just like Pictionary, hosting isn't about showing off our drawing skills, it's about drawing something people can recognise and care about in an instant. It doesn't matter how clever our questions are, how smooth our delivery is, or how sharp our guest sounds. If the host, the guest, and the audience aren't seeing the same picture, the whole thing falls apart. Before anything else, we've got to zoom out, get out of the detail of the run sheet, and consider the bigger picture.

What's this really about? What connects everyone in the room? What is the throughline? How will I *draw* that? How can I spotlight the shared purpose that makes this worth showing up for? And with that single word – purpose – I'm starting to sound like a self-help author, so let's go there, eh?

Simon Sinek made waves (and thousands of dollars) with one simple phrase: *Start with why.* He didn't mean go full existential. He meant: don't just explain *what* you're doing, make it clear *why* it matters. He argued that great leaders don't inspire action with spreadsheets or dot points. They do it by anchoring people to a purpose. That's what grabs attention. That's what sticks (Sinek, 2009).

Hosting is no different. When we can identify why the conversation will matter to each person in the room – each cog – we'll get them turning in sync.

"Circle!" "Clock!". Meanwhile, our team's yelling out almost the complete opposite, "Square!" "Cross" "Flag" "Union Jack!" Then, "London!"

The answer is London. We won. I distinctly remember Mum turning to my uncle, looking down at what he'd drawn, and saying, "Well, what's that?"

"It's Big Ben!" he said, referring to the clock tower that stands in the middle of London. And it was. It was a masterpiece of miniature architecture, drawn in under a minute. But it didn't help Mum get to "London."

That's what I call a calibration fail. It's when we get too busy thinking about everything we know and care about, and not enough time thinking about what our audience and guests know and care about. So we end up drawing Big Ben and wonder why no one 'gets it'.

This happens in hosting all the time. We overcook the structure, we look for big-name guests, we polish every transition, lock in our questions, finesse the script, but forget to ask: is this going to land for the person on the other end?

A beautifully run event that doesn't spark a real connection is just Big Ben in a board game. Technically impressive, but useless in the moment. That's why calibration matters. Before we can make it good, we have to make it work.

The Three Essentials of Calibration

There are three things you can do to calibrate well:

- Consider the whole picture: getting the host, guest, and audience in sync.
- Tune into the audience's perspective: knowing what they need, expect, and care about.

Three cogs that need to turn in sync to reach an end goal. If one's out of alignment, the whole thing feels off.

Calibration is about checking the cogs are in alignment before we crank the handle. It's making sure your energy, your content, and your approach match the moment and the people in it.

Because when it's off, you feel it. Things get clunky. The audience isn't quite with you. The guest doesn't settle in. The whole thing feels like more effort than it should. When things are out of alignment, it doesn't matter how well you deliver, because it's not a delivery issue, it's a calibration issue.

The first time I realised how important calibration is, I was playing a game of Pictionary.

The Pictionary Problem: A Lesson in Calibration

My mum was a terrible Pictionary player. So bad that we'd all 'bags not' be her partner. If you haven't played, Pictionary is a board game where you team up in pairs, then one person draws a picture, while the other guesses what's being drawn. The faster you get the answer right, the faster you move around the board.

One summer at the beach, my uncle came to visit. He's an architect and a brilliant drawer. Mum's eyes lit up the moment she saw him and quickly bagsed him as her Pictionary partner. She was very pleased with herself and felt pretty sure she'd finally get a win on the board.

That night, we all sat down to play, and the first round was an 'All Play'. This means every team is drawing, every team is guessing, all at once. It gets loud quickly, but it also means you can (accidentally) cheat by listening to what others are yelling out. But it doesn't always help...

As things kicked off, I could hear Mum yelling out things like

- **Prepare**: set the space, consider the roles, and focus on the vibe so you can establish resonance quickly.

Miss one, and things go sideways. Nail all three? That's when hosting becomes effortless. This section will show you how to do just that, starting with *The Calibration*, where we make sure everything fits just right before anyone walks into the room.

The Calibration – Make It Work Before You Make It Good

Why Calibration Matters

It's easy to spend time on the wrong things when trying to become a better host. I've done it. You've done it. Anyone who's hosted anything has done it. We obsess over how we sound, whether we'll say the right thing, whether we'll get laughs or look clever, whether the tech will behave and if we've got the perfect introduction. We think if we just prepare more, script better, or refine our delivery, we'll be the perfect host. And sure, those things help, but they don't make us great hosts.

Other times, we forget the prep altogether and fall back on our natural charm, the guest's expertise, or the 'natural vibe', hoping they will carry us through. Sometimes we fixate on one part of the experience, crafting a killer intro for our audience, or obsessing over questions for our guest, but we forget that hosting isn't about any one piece.

If we think of the show, event or meeting as a machine, like any machine, it only runs well when the parts are working together. Hosting is a three-part system: the host, the guest, and the audience.

Hosting is a three-part system: the host, the guest, and the audience. Three cogs that need to turn in sync to reach an end goal. If one's out of alignment, the whole thing feels off.

bits that carry weight. It's not just fact-checking, but ordering chaos into coherence, to find the narrative spine. You can hear it in the flow of every episode. Even when it sounds casual, there's a current pulling you forward.

Finally, there's the art of his preparation. He doesn't just read the notes. He lets them marinate, then pays attention to what sparks his own interest. He says, "if you can reconnect with your inner eight-year-old — the one who still wonders why the sky is blue — you start noticing what really matters again." I love this so much. That's what gets him ready; not a tight script, but a curious mind and a clear structure in his head.

For me, it's structure that gives a host freedom. It's what lets them pause mid-conversation and say, "Wait, what did you just say?" Not because they're lost or confused, but because they've become *lost* in the story and are genuinely *with* the guest and are experiencing each surprise at the same time as the audience.

Reading this conversation between two of the industry greats felt like both validation and confirmation about what it takes to get ready to host something. Tools and instincts. Phew. Thank you, Leigh and Richard, great to know we're on the same page!

Your Prep Work

There are three parts to good hosting prep, and they all build on each other:

- **Calibrate**: align the content, audience, and structure so everything fits together.
- **Curate**: select the content that will help the conversation land.

What Richard Fidler Taught Me About Preparation

I once sat next to Richard Fidler on a bus. He's a journalist, long time radio host, chart-topping podcaster, Doug Anthony All Star, and well known to Australian audiences.

The trip was about 30 minutes long, on our way to the ABC showcase at Parliament House in Canberra. As I got up, I remember feeling like our chat was a story worth archiving at the National Library! I'd mentioned I was from Tasmania and he immediately launched into a memory of a man who ran a hotel in Penguin where every room had its own quirky theme. He effortlessly moved between sharing stories and asking questions. He was thoughtful, funny, and entirely tuned in. In those 30 minutes, I learned a lot. However, the information I received wasn't just about the people in the stories he told, I also learned about him, and somehow, also about me. How did he do that?

But it wasn't on the bus that I really started learning from him. That happened later, reading *Storytellers* by Leigh Sales – another big name in the Australian media hosting scene.

There's a chapter in her book that gives a behind-the-scenes look at how Fidler approaches his work on his radio show and podcast, *Conversations*. As I read, I kept finding myself both nodding along and wanting to high-five someone because what I read felt like validation of the kind of preparation I've always believed in.

Fidler talks about how the show is a 'beast to feed,' yet every guest is chosen deliberately, not just for who they are, but for the shape of their story. The first step is searching for something his audience can grasp onto. He's not looking for status, he's looking for substance. I call this calibration.

Then comes the curation stage. His producers do long pre-interviews, helping the guest sift through their own life to find the

Before

Setting Up to Host Well

It's impossible to be a great host without having a clear understanding of what we're hosting, who it's for, and why it matters. Sounds obvious, I know. But finding out these details is surprisingly easy to skip. We get caught up in the mechanics, what to say, how to sound, whether we've got the tech right... all while overlooking the one thing that matters most: *who is this for and why does it matter to them?*

Great hosts do this work long before the mic is on or the agenda is set. Not with a script. Not with an opening joke. But with the three questions that shape everything else:

- What are you hosting: what's the purpose and tone of this conversation?
- Who are you hosting for: who needs to engage, and what matters to them right now?
- How will you make it matter: so the event, podcast, panel, or meeting feels impossible to ignore?

Great Toast: The Balance You're Aiming For

The strongest hosts aren't the loudest or flashiest. They're the ones who know when to lean in and when to lean out. They've got structure, but don't stick to the script. They can lift the energy or steady the space. They make people feel seen without needing to be centre stage.

Hosting like this starts by noticing your default settings and asking, is this intentional or just a habit I've picked up along the way? Because sometimes the habits that keep us "in control" actually stop connection. And what you *intend* to do doesn't always match how people *experience* you. Great Toast hosts know the difference.

You don't have to start from scratch. You already have some great instincts and tools, we perhaps just need to sharpen them.

I've no doubt that your hosting habits shift depending on the space, the stakes, and who's in the room. If you'd like to find out how you're currently showing up and what might need a tweak, scan the QR code and take my quick quiz. It'll show you what's working, what's getting in the way, and how to fine-tune your presence for real impact.

Very few people share
spreadsheets at the pub.
They share stories.

What We Know

Facts are forgettable unless we wrap them in something worth caring about. As Carmine Gallo puts it, storytelling isn't just the fluff to add in after the data, it's how we *make sense* of the data. He watched hundreds of TED Talks, tallied up the techniques, and found one clear pattern: the talks people remembered most weren't the ones packed with data, they were the ones packed with meaning. Specifically, with stories. Stats alone might earn a nod but a story earns a memory (Gallo, 2014). Which is why I run whole programs helping people take their sharpest facts or high-level concepts and wrap them in meaning, because the truth is, very few people share spreadsheets at the pub. They share stories.

The Cost

- The audience tunes out because the room feels cold, even if the content is good.
- Conversations feels transactional, informative, but forgettable. Nothing changes.
- Your events all blur into one another.

The Fix

- Shift from facts to feeling: data matters, but so does connection.
- Loosen up: let your personality come through, even in technical discussions.
- Make it about the audience: focus on what they care about, not just what you want to cover.

The Great Toast Theory

The Fix

- Stop treating 'the host' as a character you need to play and start seeing 'the host' as you. You may need to learn how to be yourself in the hosting seat, rather than learning how to be what you think is expected.
- Prioritise depth over drama. One great moment of connection is better than five one-liners.
- Shift the spotlight. Your job is to shape, not dominate.

Dry Toast: The Emotionally Disconnected Host

Technically correct. Emotionally absent. They've done the reading, they've got the facts, but they forgot the vibe. Dry Toast hosts walk people through agendas, data, and frameworks like they're teaching a statistics class to people who didn't sign up for it.

They stick to the facts, deliver precise information, and follow the agenda perfectly, but they don't make it matter. Instead of drawing people in, they push words out. Instead of creating a moment, they run through the motions.

Could This Be You?

- You tell everyone what's on the program, but forget to tell them why it's important.
- You finish every segment with, "Any questions?" and get silence.
- You have well-researched questions but only get safe answers, not real ones.
- You present all the right statistics, but forget to tell a story that makes people care about them.

Could This Be You?

- You ask questions that sound like a performance, leaving your guest or group unsure if you're actually interested in their answer.
- You keep jumping in with your own take, hoping to sound sharp, but it comes off like you're correcting or outshining the people you invited to speak.
- You feel the need to bring 'the vibe,' so you crank up the energy instead of tuning in to what's needed.
- You walk away buzzing, but your guest (or team) is left wondering if their voice really mattered.

What We Know

There's a fine line between charisma and performance. Amy Cuddy, alongside Matthew Kohut and John Neffinger, describes this as the warmth-competence trade-off. Turns out, when we're too busy trying to look competent, we often forget to be warm, and that's the bit people trust. They found we're more likely to trust someone who feels warm and relatable than someone who seems all polish and performance (Cuddy, Kohut, and Neffinger, 2013).

The Cost

- The audience feels like they're being talked at rather than invited into a conversation.
- The guest or group feels like a prop rather than the focus of the discussion.
- People remember the performance rather than the content of the conversation.

The Great Toast Theory

The Cost
- The audience struggles to stay engaged because the conversation feels chaotic.
- The guests feel like they're doing all the work, trying to make sense of vague, wandering questions.
- The host loses credibility because they seem unsure, unstructured, or unprepared.

The Fix
- Ask one clear question at a time. Long, layered questions only confuse people.
- Know the purpose of the conversation. If you're not clear, they won't be either.
- Keep the goal in sight. Gently steer things back when they go off track.
- Don't fear the silence. Give your guest space to think and speak.

Slick Toast: The Over-Performer

They sound impressive. They look confident. They're smooth. Maybe too smooth. Something feels... off. Everything has a polished edge, like they're delivering a conference keynote instead of hosting a conversation. It's all sparkle, no soul. All energy, no intimacy. The audience might clap and laugh, but they don't properly connect. And the guest is left feeling like they are the understudy in someone else's show.

Raw Toast: The Waffler

This host means well. You can see the good intentions, and sometimes even glimmers of gold, but it's wrapped in a roll of ramble. Sometimes, they land brilliant, raw moments of emotion, but because they haven't put in the structure or prep, those moments are hit-or-miss.

Their questions wander. Their intros meander. They start a sentence, shift directions mid-way, then land somewhere else entirely. Their guest(s) is left thinking, "Wait, what was the question again?"

Could This Be You?

- You ask vague, open-ended questions and then don't know what to do with the answers.
- You let conversations run in circles without shaping them into decisions, perspectives, or stories.
- You apologise for asking questions instead of just asking them.
- You allow discussions to become echo chambers rather than action makers.

What We Know

Structure doesn't kill spontaneity; it rescues it from becoming a waffle. Study after study shows that a few clear guideposts keep us steady without becoming stiff. When people know what's coming, they relax. When you know what you're doing, you stop gripping the mic like a flotation device. Communication researcher Sarah Chesebro found that clear structure makes audiences feel less anxious and more engaged, and it actually boosts your credibility too (Chesebro and McCroskey, 2001). So, if your tendency is to ramble, maybe it's not about polish but planning.

- You focus so much on a perfect delivery, you forget to connect.
- You play it safe. You want to get the job done without conflict, emotion, or risk.

What We Know

You could open just about any article on communication and they'll all say the same thing: people trust *authenticity* more than *perfection.* A slight stumble? A genuine pause to think? A laugh that wasn't planned? That's what makes people lean in. When it's too smooth, we make people suspicious. While we know this, are we ready to allow it?

Amy Cuddy puts it beautifully in *Presence* (2015). She found that when we're focused on getting everything right – every word, every pause, every eyebrow – we're not *in* the moment. We're managing it. And when you're managing the moment, and trying to be the boss of it, you're not really part of it. You might sound impressive. But you'll feel distant. And so will your audience.

The Cost

- Our audience zones out because we sound too robotic, rehearsed, or safe.
- Our guests don't feel guided, they feel managed.
- The energy in the room flatlines because it feels forced.

The Fix

- Ditch the full script. Use key ideas, not paragraphs.
- Go looking for surprises instead of fearing them.
- Focus on creating space for a conversation to happen, rather than controlling it.

A slight stumble? A genuine pause to think? A laugh that wasn't planned? That's what makes people lean in. When it's too smooth, we make people suspicious. While we know this, are we ready to allow it?

The Four Types of Bad Toast Hosts

You know these people. You've seen these people. You've been these people. We all have at different times in our lives. It's when we forget what the audience is asking for and we just settle back into our habits.

Most hosts don't know their default, but the moment you see yourself in one of these, you can fix it. So, let's break them down, because the difference between unpalatable and phenomenal is just a few small shifts on the dial.

Burnt Toast: The Over-Scripted Host

You know that feeling when someone sounds like they're reading straight from a teleprompter? They're so polished, it feels like a recital. No detours. No real presence. Every question lands like a checklist item. That's Burnt Toast.

This host is so prepared that they can somehow squeeze the life out of a very real-life moment. They're the ones who say everything right but feel all wrong. Their cue cards have cue cards! They're following their script so rigidly that they miss the actual moment happening in front of them. And if the energy in the room shifts? They don't.

Could This Be You?
- You stick to your plan even when the room clearly wants to go somewhere else.
- You ask the questions on the list, in order, without connecting one to the next, draining the energy from the room and the authenticity from your face.

a seemingly normal man lose it at the continental breakfast bar. He kept putting his toast in and at first, it came out barely warm. He sent it through again, and then it came out burnt to a crisp.

He threw up his hands, swore at the machine, sighed deeply, then turned to me and said, "Why can't they build a toaster that gets this right?" There was no judgment from me, only empathy. I get it. It feels like there are only a few milliseconds between toast that's underdone and toast that's overdone – it's a tricky balance.

After working with hundreds of leaders, experts, and advocates, I know that just because you've spent years speaking, leading meetings, or running events, it doesn't mean you'll come out the other side a great host.

Some are overdone – too stiff, too scripted, too unnatural. Some are undercone – rambling, unclear, or hard to follow. Then they try to fix it with 'toppings.' Some lay it on too thick – all style, no substance, too polished to be real. Some are too dry – technically correct, but lacking warmth or connection. We've all seen bad toast. The ones who talk too much. The ones who say almost nothing. The ones who overperform. The ones who just don't connect.

So, I decided to build the toaster.

This book is the toaster. It's designed to help you identify your default settings and then tweak the dial to get that perfect balance – where you're prepared but natural, confident but relatable, structured but spontaneous.

Because when you get it right? You become a Great Toast Host – engaging, impactful, and impossible to ignore. So, let's find out your current default settings.

The Great Toast Theory

You now know that hosting isn't just about turning up and hoping for the best. You know it takes tools and it takes instincts. You've started to think about what it's going to take to move past the Tool Checkpoint, to stop guessing and start using tools that work for you. And you've probably got your eye on the Frequency Line too, where your instinct, rhythm, and presence all click into place. You'll build your toolkit. You'll tune your instincts. You've started to think about what you can do before, during and after, so you've got a hosting strategy that works for you.

But here's what we haven't figured out yet: what happens by default when you find yourself hosting a conversation?

When it's your turn to run the room, hold the mic, and guide the conversation, what habits kick in? What instincts lead? What tone do you set without even realising it? Because before we build your strategy, we need to get clear on your default settings.

And that... is where the toaster comes in.

The Toaster

Have you ever yelled at a toaster? I have. There's nothing more frustrating than the ones you find in a hotel buffet. I once watched

From Making It Up to Making It Matter   19

So clever phrases? No. But clever phases? Yes. That's what this book is about. Breaking the craft of hosting into three simple phases: *Before*, *During*, and *After*, and sharing practical tools, insider information, and mindset shifts to sharpen how you lead conversations.

If you only prepare but don't guide the room, you'll be forgettable. If you show up well but don't follow up, you'll lose momentum. If you only focus on follow-up... hang on, who even does that? You know who. It's the hosts who misrepresent reality online, quickly losing trust.

But if you master all three? You'll be the host who gets more out of a single moment than most people get from an entire campaign. You'll shape the moment, amplify the message, and build the kind of reputation that lasts. But before we get to that, we need to talk about toast. Yep, toast.

However, the best results come when hosts can focus on assessing and adjusting the energy.

Where most hosts get stuck:

- They tighten up under pressure and race through their content.
- They dominate the mic instead of guiding the conversation.
- They go flat. Even with great prep, their presence doesn't land.
- They overperform and miss the chance to really connect.
- They don't adapt when the energy shifts, so the room slips away.

The *During* section gives you nine ways to lift the energy, read the moment, and create conversations that resonate.

After: Turning One Conversation Into Many

The most common mistake hosts make is thinking their job is done when the conversation ends. The best hosts know how to make their work continue to work, long after the moment has passed.

Where most hosts drop the ball:

- They don't follow up, so the connection fades.
- They don't repurpose the work, so it disappears after the event.
- They don't reflect, so they repeat the same patterns.

The *After* section gives you nine ways to extend your impact, build trust, and make sure every conversation keeps working long after it ends.

The most common mistake
hosts make is thinking
their job is done when the
conversation ends.

To be the kind of host people trust, remember, and love, you need to do all three:

- Before: set the conditions for a great conversation.
- During: create resonance intentionally and continually.
- After: cement the impact, so it lasts beyond the moment.

Skip one, and things get clunky. Nail all three, and people will seek you out again and again.

Before: Setting Yourself Up for Success

By now, you've realised that the job of hosting doesn't start when the room fills or the mic goes live. It starts much earlier.

Where most hosts go wrong:

- They underprepare, relying on confidence instead of context.
- They overprepare, scripting every word until there's no room to move.
- They forget about the audience and make the session about their plan, not the people in the room.

The *Before* section of this book gives you nine tools to help you tune in, prep well, and walk in with clarity, calm, and confidence.

During: Keep the Room Alive

Preparation sets you up, but what happens in the room is what people remember. Most hosts struggle here because they get focused on their carefully prepared agenda or list of questions.

that are already sitting inside you and show you how to use them to build energy, create connection, and bring people together.

Evolutionary science tells us that humans didn't survive because we were the fastest or the strongest; we made it because we knew how to collaborate. Our ability to cooperate, communicate, and find common ground is what got us this far. We just forget sometimes. Or get in our own way. This book is about helping you remember how to do it, your way. Let's get into the strategy.

The Strategy

Most people think hosting is about what happens in the moment. They picture a charismatic speaker, a sharp interviewer, or a comedic moderator who magically holds everyone's attention.

That's only one-third of the job. There are three parts to good hosting strategy, and I reckon most people have a bias for one and a blind spot for the others.

Some think preparation is everything, so they plan every detail. They script their introductions, over-engineer their transitions, and map out every question. But the second things go off-script, they panic like a wombat on a highway.

Some believe it's all about the moment and trust themselves to just wing it. They improvise, vibe it out, and hope the conversation will go somewhere useful. But because they haven't set the conditions for success, they spend the whole time playing catch-up.

And no one ever thinks about what happens after. They run the session, tick the box, and move on. No reflection. No relationship-building. No ripple effect. Then they rinse and repeat the same mistakes.

Host in a way that feels
unmistakably you.

The Tool Checkpoint. Once you cross this, you start gathering (or borrowing) the tools that you need and ditching the ones you don't. You're building a bespoke tool kit filled with structures you've tested, habits you've built and rituals that actually work for you.

The second is the Frequency Line. This is when your instincts are sharp and you trust them. The tools live in your body, not just your notes. You're able to tune into the frequencies of your guests and your audience, and then get everyone on the same wavelength.

If you're feeling ineffective, inconsistent, or like you're stuck somewhere between good intentions and flat conversations, you're not alone. Most people never get past those early steps because they've never been taught how hosting actually works. The difference between a host who reacts and a host who resonates lies in the craft - in tools that fit and instincts that are finely tuned.

This book will help you find them.

What You'll Get From this Book

If you're looking for a list of one-liners or plug-and-play intro phrases, I'm going to disappoint you. This isn't that kind of book. Soz. One thing I know for sure is you don't need *my* words; we need *yours*.

This book is about giving you the strategy, structure, and some suggestions that will help you to host in a way that feels unmistakably you.

If there's one thing I've learned from audiences, whether in studios, stages, workshops, or meetings, it's that humans have excellent bullshit detectors. They can tell when you're not being real and when that happens, they switch off.

So instead of teaching you a heap of new tricks, I'm going to help you use what you already have, but better. We'll uncover the skills

The Shift to Make: You've found your voice. Help others find theirs.

The Tool to Use: *In Reflection* – use this process to decode what makes your hosting work, so you can teach it, model it, and multiply your impact.

What This Means for You

FUEL: What's driving you.	FEELING: How you feel.	FREQUENCY: How are you received.
OBLIGATION You're showing up out of duty, not design.	INEFFECTIVE You feel unnecessary. like you're taking up space rather than shaping it.	REACTIVE You're reacting, not responding.
OVERWHELM You're trying too hard, holding too tight.	INCONSISTENT You're passionate but frustrated.	RESISTANT You're controlling instead of flowing.
OPENNESS You're starting to listen, adapt and co-create.	INTENTIONAL You're understanding the importance of your role.	RESPONSIVE You're tuned in and adjusting in real time.
ORIGINALITY You're leading with your own style and voice.	IMPACTFUL You feel the trust from others to guide the conversation.	REFINED You speak with clarity, rhythm, and ease.
OPPORTUNITY You're hosting to lift others, not yourself.	INFLUENTIAL Your known presence shifts the energy.	RESONANT You read the room and can manage any moment.

So, where do you fit on here? Better yet, where do you want to be?

You'll notice there are two big lines on this map. The first, I call

From Making It Up to Making It Matter 11

You're not mimicking other hosts. You're not defaulting to a run sheet. You're starting to trust your instincts. Your voice has shape. Your presence has pace. You've stopped focusing on keeping things moving and started focusing on making them matter.

At this stage, originality is driving you. You're hosting with clarity, nuance, and tone that feels *uniquely yours*. And that's what makes people listen. They come for the space you hold and how you shape it.

The Shift to Make: Don't be tempted by someone else's script. Start hosting in a way that only you can.

The Tool to Use: *The Rituals* – this helps you develop daily deliberate practices that keep your energy aligned and your hosting fresh, grounded, and distinct.

5. You're powered by opportunity, feel influential, and are resonant.

You're not just navigating; you're guiding others through the dark.

You've become the host people think of first. They've noticed that you create a stage for others, rather than claiming its centre. You've got a presence that goes far beyond performance and into possibility.

You guide conversations that change how people think, feel, and act. You help others shine. You elevate their voices, shaping the space for their stories to land and creating moments that matter for the speaker and the listener alike.

At this stage, opportunity is driving you. Not for yourself, but for the people you're holding space for. Hosting becomes an act of service. You know it's not about running the room but finding resonance.

The tool to use: *The Curation* — to filter the fluff, read the room, and hold attention without gripping the mic too tight.

3. You approach with openness, feel intentional, and stay responsive in the moment.

You're experimenting, navigating by feel with a compass you trust.

You've started to crack the code and are relaxing into your role. Hosting isn't something that happens *to* you anymore; you're actively shaping it.

You come prepared, but you're not performing. You listen deeply. You know when to pause, when to pivot, when to push. You're no longer simply reacting to the room; you're responding with intention.

At this stage, openness is driving you. You're ready to co-create the sh*t out of this conversation! And that presence? It creates trust. To put it more bluntly, you've finally started showing up, instead of showing off. That's a huge change.

The Shift to Make: Keep focusing on the *craft*, not just the content. Experiment. Adjust. Let the conversation breathe.

The Tool to Use: *The Preparation* — master the space, pace, and resonance so your energy invites engagement without forcing it.

4. You're fuelled by originality, feel impactful, and come across as refined.

Hosting with tools and instincts that feel like yours and work like magic.

You've put in the reps. You've learned the frameworks, built your confidence, found your rhythm, and now you're leaning into your own way of doing things.

From Making It Up to Making It Matter   9

is flat, the engagement is patchy, and the results are forgettable. You know this because you need to send follow-up emails and chase people up, or you don't see any audience response post-show.

Right now, obligation is driving you. You're showing up out of duty, not design. You assume hosting is just part of your position description, and requires you to speak clearly, and follow the agenda. But deep down, you know something's missing. You know the conversation isn't connecting. You know it's a bad look.

The Shift to Make: Stop thinking of hosting as talking. Start seeing it as creating the conditions for connection.

The Tool to Use: *The Calibration* — your guide to setting up conversations that make people lean in, not check out.

2. You're fuelled by overwhelm, feel inconsistent, and appear resistant.

You've loaded your backpack with tools that aren't set up for you.

You've started taking the role seriously. You're hosting meetings or panels or podcasts, and sometimes, it clicks. Other times? It tanks. You leave unsure of what just happened.

You prep hard. You try to get everything right. But in doing so, you resist the energy in the room. You stick to scripts when it needs spontaneity. You try and control when the moment needs curiosity. And the more you try, the less it lands.

Right now, overwhelm is driving you. You care deeply, but it's too much. Maybe it's too much about you? And your energy? It's resisting the moment. You're holding too tight, and not letting the moment breathe.

The Shift to Make: Stop trying to control every variable. Start tuning in to what the moment actually needs.

Some people are all about the tools. They've got the questions, the structures, the strategies, maybe even a colour-coded run sheet. But the second the conversation veers off track? Panic. They're standing there, compass in hand, watching the map fly off in the wind.

Others are all instinct. They trust their gut, they read the room, they respond in the moment. But when they need to land a key message or bring a discussion back on track? Nothing. Just echolocating wildly, hoping they don't crash into a wall or another bat.

Either way, you've probably felt it: something isn't quite working. Maybe you've run meetings that feel like one-way broadcasts; people are there, but not really there. Maybe some conversations click and others fall flat, and you can't quite figure out why. Maybe you've got strong instincts but no structure, or great preparation but zero flexibility when things shift.

So how do you know where you stand? In the pages ahead, you'll get a snapshot of what's fuelling you, how it feels in the role, and how you're being received. You'll also be pointed straight to the parts of this book that should go straight into your kit to help you shift from making it up... to making it matter.

1. You're driven by obligation, feel ineffective, and come across as reactive.

You're running the room without a map or internal compass.

You don't really think of yourself as a host. You started a podcast because it felt like something you *should* do. You run meetings because it's part of your job. You guide conversations, ask the questions, follow the agenda, and hope everything lands.

But it doesn't. Conversations drift. Guests ramble. Attendees check out. You're talking, but no one's really leaning in. The energy

From Making It Up to Making It Matter

What are you doing right now as a host? Are you making it up or making it matter? The difference between them has little to do with natural talent and much more to do with the content of your hosting kit. We all come with one built in; however, it's often been filled up with tools and instincts that aren't that useful. Chances are no one has taught you what you'll need or how to pack it. Both are essential bits of knowledge if you want to be a better host.

Building Your Kit

What's in your hosting kit right now? When it's your job to shape the moment, whether you're leading a meeting, a podcast, a panel, a workshop, or a tough conversation, what are you actually working with? What's driving you when the spotlight's on? What are you relying on when things go off script? What instincts do you rely on? What tools have you got?

As the host, I had to navigate two different audiences at the same time:

- The people in the room.
- The listeners at home.

I had to juggle guest interviews, performances, weather crosses, newsroom updates, and even talkback callers, all while keeping the energy high and the show on track.

It was a constant dance between orienteering and echolocation. Like an orienteer along with my team, we had prepared the guests, mapped the show, we had the tools for the job and planned the key transitions. Like a bat, I was receiving live feedback — body language, audience laughter, the rhythm of the show, and breaking news — and adjusting to what was unfolding in the moment.

At the same time, I was managing behind-the-scenes elements: receiving updates from my producer, monitoring audience engagement online, and coordinating with my technical team.

This is full Or enteering Bat mode; navigating the moment with both tools and instinct. And that's exactly what I want to help you do in this book.

It turns out, I've been using echolocation this whole time. But that wasn't the only time I recognised my craft in another.

Every year, I'd interview either a president of an orienteering club or a top competitor ahead of their big annual event. I'd listen as they described how the orienteers prepared, how they'd study maps, understand the terrain, and anticipate obstacles before even setting foot on the course. Unlike bats, who rely on internal systems, orienteers use external tools — maps, compasses, and strategies — so they can navigate confidently, no matter what gets thrown in their way. Again, I thought, that's a bit like what I do as a host.

That's when I realised a great host needs to be both; an orienteer and a bat.

Like a bat, we need to be constantly sending and receiving signals, picking up on cues from our guests, reading the energy in the room, noticing the shape of the space, and adapting in real time. It's an internal system built on instinct.

Like an orienteer, we need to have done our prep, knowing our guests, understanding our audience, and having a solid map of where we're headed, even if we take a few unexpected detours. We need external tools.

Master both, and we can shape conversation from the inside out.

Hosting in Action

I spent ten years as a live radio presenter, and one of my favourite gigs was a radio show we broadcast live each year from the Devonport Jazz Festival. It became a ticketed event, blending live interviews, performances, and audience interaction from the room, along with radio show staples like weather crosses, traffic reports, and news bulletins, all while being broadcast on the radio to listeners at home.

in such a way that it helps others uncover insights they didn't even know they had. The kind that shifts thinking and changes minds. Woah, that feels big. It's not really.

It's just about remembering that a great host connects things – people to ideas, people to people, and ideas to ideas, and everything and everyone to a bigger purpose.

So yes, it is bigger than 'just running a meeting', it's about shaping moments. It's more than leading conversations, it's about creating momentum. And in doing so, a host becomes the kind of person people turn to. The kind of leader others trust.

Now that is the real power of hosting. So how do you do it? Pfft, easy! You become an Orienteering Bat, obviously.

What Bats and Orienteers Can Teach Us About Hosting

I don't often identify with characters in David Attenborough documentaries, but once, I did. I was watching a segment about bats — yes, the tiny, winged creatures that dart through the darkness — when he explained their secret: echolocation.

He explained that bats don't rely on sight to find their way. Instead, they send out high-frequency sounds that bounce back, giving them a detailed picture of their environment. That's how they navigate, avoiding obstacles and constantly adjusting to what's ahead. As I listened, something clicked, or maybe bounced back...

That's exactly how I feel as a host! The moment the conversation starts, which is usually long before I press record or step on stage, I'm sending out signals — questions, comments, reactions, expressions — waiting for something to bounce back. I'm listening, not just to words, but to tone, rhythm, context, hesitation, and excitement. I'm mapping the space between us, picking up on what's clear and what's still hidden, adjusting my path as I go.

Introduction

We're all hosting every day.

- In team briefings, boardrooms, and one-on-one conversations that determine engagement, retention, and impact.
- In advocacy spaces, community discussions, and campaigns where the right message can drive real change.
- In email threads and discussions, where momentum is either made or lost.
- In interviews, pitches, and presentations, where ideas either land or get overlooked.

And yet, most of us aren't hosting as well as we could. The cost of that?

- Low engagement: audiences, employees, and even top leaders check out.
- Missed opportunities: brilliant ideas never surface, and innovation stalls.
- Lost trust and credibility: people don't turn to us when it matters.
- Untapped potential: hidden talent, solutions, and insights remain buried.
- Decisions that don't stick because people weren't truly engaged in the process.

We often think of hosts as facilitators, guiding a process, keeping things on track. But for me, it's more active than that. It's not only about holding space, but helping shape it. Great hosts work with what's in the room: the energy, the dynamics, the content, the people. They set the conditions for connection, where people feel safe enough to share, heard enough to contribute, and sparked enough to act. They do more than pass the mic, they hand it over

Introduction

O f all the questions I was asked about my job as a radio host, the most common was, "What time do you get to work?" Not, "How do you keep a conversation flowing?" Not, "What makes an interview unforgettable?" Not even, "How do you make guests feel comfortable?" Just, "What time do you get to work?"

As it turns out, most people assumed I turned up a few minutes before going on air, walked into the studio, turned on the mic, and began talking. If only!

What I've learned is that while most hear and see hosts doing their thing, very few understand what goes into their thing. And I think that's a problem. Hosting isn't just for radio presenters, podcasters and event MCs. It's for leaders, experts, and changemakers; anyone who needs to bring people together, shape conversations, make ideas stick and travel. We're all hosting every day:

- In face-to-face and online meetings where decisions are shaped, strategies are set, and cultures are built.
- On podcasts, panels, and in workshops that can position us as credible experts worth following.

Contents

Introduction 1

From Making It Up to Making It Matter 7
Building Your Kit 7
The Strategy 15

The Great Toast Theory 21
The Four Types of Bad Toast Hosts 23
Great Toast: The Balance You're Aiming For 32

Before 33
The Calibration – Make It Work Before You Make It Good 37
The Curation – How to Find and Sort Ideas Before You Need Them . . . 48
The Preparation – Tuning the Situation, Relationship, and Vibe 56
Before You Start, Set the Stage and Set Yourself 69

During 71
The Rituals – The Secret to Feeling Ready, Every Time 74
The Rapport Card – Scoring High on Connection in Every
    Conversation 83
The Route – Questions that Take You Somewhere Real 92
Where the Mic Comes Alive 110

After 111
The Share – Shaping How Your Hosting Is Remembered 113
The Art of Asking – How the Right Questions Turn Moments into
    Movements 121
In Reflection – The Final Three Steps to Hosting Brilliance 128
What Happens After Is What Makes You Better 138

Conclusion 139
Then vs. Now 140
Keep Hosting 143

References 145

Copyright © 2025 Penny Terry

All rights reserved. No part of this publication may be reproduced, distributed, or transmitted in any form or by any means, including photocopying, recording, or other electronic or mechanical methods, without the prior written permission of the publisher, except in the case of brief quotations embodied in critical reviews and certain other noncommercial uses permitted by copyright law.

Every effort has been made to trace and seek permission for the use of the original source material used within this book. Where the attempt has been unsuccessful, the publisher would be pleased to hear from the author/publisher to rectify any omission

First publishec in 2025 by Hambone Publishing
www.hambonepublishing.com.au

 A catalogue record for this book is available from the National Library of Australia

Editing by Mish Phillips, Lexi Wight and Emily Stephenson
Cover desigr by I SAW A PLATYPUS
Interior design by David W. Edelstein

For information about this title, contact:
Penny Terry
penny@pennyterry.com

ISBN 978-1-922357-71-7 (paperback)
ISBN 978-1-922357-72-4 (ebook)

BE A BETTER HOST

THE MIC DROP

HOW TO CREATE THE CONDITIONS THAT MAKE EVERY PODCAST, MEETING AND EVENT RESONATE

Penny Terry

About the Author

Penny Terry has spent more than two decades behind microphones and on stages, shaping, sharing, and shifting conversations that matter. A former ABC Radio presenter, she has interviewed more than 20,000 people, hosted and produced award-winning podcasts, and learned firsthand what makes messages land and what makes them fall flat.

No matter which side of the mic you're on, Penny has lived it in real time. She has experienced what works, studied the evidence, and built clear, practical strategies to help people get better. Today she works with executive leaders, experts, and change makers, helping them share who they are, what they know, and why it matters.

Whether you're asking the questions or answering them, Penny helps you shape the narrative, share it well, and shift what's possible. Because it's not enough to be right, you have to resonate.

Acknowledgement of Country

It would be impossible for me to write a book full of stories without being moved and inspired by the traditions of First Nations cultures.

I acknowledge the palawa/pakana peoples, the Traditional Owners of Lutruwita/Tasmania. I pay my respects to Elders past and present and extend that respect to all First Nations peoples across Australia.

I acknowledge the storytellers and knowledge keepers whose stories are so powerful and so enduring that they have carried vital knowledge of culture, community, and Country through countless generations, sustaining the world's oldest continuous cultures.

I am often reminded of the wisdom in these stories as I walk through the landscapes of Lutruwita/Tasmania. They ground me in the understanding that I live, learn, and work on Country, and they remind me of the responsibility I carry when I share stories of my own.

Be a Better Host

If you're wondering which side of this book is the front, the answer depends on what you want to learn. Open it this way and you're in the host's chair. Flip it over and you're in the guest's seat. Both sides share the same DNA, and as such, some similar words and lessons, but the focus shifts depending on which side of the mic you're on.

As a host, your job is to create the conditions that make conversations resonate. This book helps you understand how you currently approach hosting, gives you a simple before–during–after strategy to follow, and offers 30 practical ways to improve each time. Learn to set things up so they work before they begin, guide the flow and manage energy, and build on each conversation so it keeps working after the mic is off.

Start here if you lead meetings, run workshops, moderate panels, or host podcasts. You'll learn to tune the room, create trust, and frame the moment so the guest shines and the audience cares. The better you host, the more you'll be recognised for the rare skill of turning conversations into catalysts — helping people share what matters in ways that shift thinking and action.

www.ingramcontent.com/pod-product-compliance
Lightning Source LLC
Chambersburg PA
CBHW061229070526
44584CB00030B/4042